Books by Conor Cruise O'Brien

PARNELL AND HIS PARTY

TO KATANGA AND BACK: A UN CASE HISTORY

MARIA CROSS: IMAGINATIVE PATTERNS IN A GROUP OF
MODERN CATHOLIC WRITERS

WRITERS AND POLITICS

THE UNITED NATIONS: SACRED DRAMA

MURDEROUS ANGELS

Murderous Angels

Murderous Angels

A POLITICAL TRAGEDY AND COMEDY
IN BLACK AND WHITE

---

by CONOR CRUISE O'BRIEN

An Atlantic Monthly Press Book
LITTLE, BROWN AND COMPANY · BOSTON · TORONTO

*No amateur or professional production of this play is permitted
without the written permission of the author.*

The lines quoted in the epigraph are from "The Tomb of
Michael Collins" from *Selected Poems* by Denis Devlin.
Copyright © 1956 by Marie C. Figarolo di Gropello. Re-
printed by permission of Holt, Rinehart and Winston, Inc.

ATLANTIC—LITTLE, BROWN BOOKS
ARE PUBLISHED BY
LITTLE, BROWN AND COMPANY
IN ASSOCIATION WITH
THE ATLANTIC MONTHLY PRESS

*Published simultaneously in Canada
by Little, Brown & Company (Canada) Limited*

PRINTED IN THE UNITED STATES OF AMERICA

IN MEMORY OF DENIS DEVLIN
(1908–1959)

And sad, Oh sad, that glen with one thin stream
He met his death in; and a farmer told me
There was but one small bird to shoot; it sang
"Better Beast and know your end, and die
Than Man with murderous angels in his head."

— DENIS DEVLIN
The Tomb of Michael Collins

Contents

Author's Preface

I

The action of this play covers the period from July 1960 to mid-September 1961, the first fifteen months, approximately, in the life of the Congo as an Independent Republic. From almost the beginning of this period up to its end (and for about two years afterwards), the United Nations was closely involved in the affairs of the Congo. On 10 July 1960, following a serious breakdown in the discipline of the Congolese Armed Forces, and the intervention of Belgian troops in the Congolese Province of Katanga, the President of the Congo, Joseph Kasavubu, and the Prime Minister, Patrice Lumumba, appealed to the United Nations for technical assistance. On 11 July 1960, Moïse Tshombe, Provincial President of Katanga, declared Katanga an independent state; this declaration was made in Elisabethville, the capital of Katanga, then occupied by Belgian paratroops. On 12 and 13 July, Kasavubu and Lumumba made new appeals to the United Nations; they now asked for military aid to protect the national territory of the Congo "against the present external aggression." On 14 July the Security Council authorized the Secretary General "to provide the Government of the Congo with such military assistance as may be necessary. . . ." The Council, having divided opinions on the subject, did not specify the purpose or purposes for which the military assistance might be necessary. On 14 and 15 July the first United Nations contingents — Ghanaian and Tunisian troops — arrived in Leopoldville.

At the time when the United Nations operation in the Congo began, I was a member of the Department of External Affairs of Ireland, with responsibility for United Nations questions. As Ireland, at the request of Secretary-General Dag Hammarskjöld, had contributed troops to the United Nations operation in the Congo, the Irish Delegation to the United Nations was represented on the Secretary-General's Advisory Committee, made up from countries actively participating in the operation. I was a representative of Ireland on the Advisory Committee. Also as a member of the Irish Delegation, I took part in the proceedings of the General Assembly when, in September 1960 after the fall of Patrice Lumumba (Act III) — that organ of the United Nations became seized of the Congo question, in consequence of the breakdown of the original consensus in the Security Council; one of the permanent members of the Council — the Soviet Union — had accused the Secretary-General of misinterpreting the Council's directives, of acting in the particular interests of the Western powers, and of interfering in the internal affairs of the Congo by helping to overthrow Prime Minister Lumumba.

On 20–21 February 1961, the consensus in the Security Council was restored, to the extent of ability to agree on the wording of a resolution; this wording was, however, subject to conflicting interpretations. This resolution authorized "the use of force if necessary in the last resort" to prevent "the occurrence of civil war in the Congo"; it also urged "measures" for the withdrawal and evacuation of foreign "military and paramilitary personnel and advisers." It was passed after a heated debate, occasioned by the news of an announcement made in Elisabethville by Godefroid Munongo, Minister of the Interior of Katanga, to the effect that Patrice Lumumba, who had been in the custody of the Katangese authorities since 17 January 1961, had met with a violent death (Acts III and IV).

Shortly after the passage of this Resolution, I was invited to join the Secretariat, for the purpose of applying the Resolution in Katanga. In April I joined the Secretariat as a director in the Division for Political and Security Council Affairs, and in May I was sent to Elisabethville, as representative of the Secretary-General in Katanga. (There are allusions to this appointment in the final scene of Act IV). I was in Elisabethville during the events which are interpreted dramatically in Act V.

In December 1961 I resigned from the service of the United Nations and of my own country, and began to write an account of my experiences which was later published under the title *To Katanga and Back* (1962). I then turned to other concerns in Ghana and later New York. In 1967, however, while at work on a book on the ritual and dramatic workings of the United Nations — now published as *The United Nations: Sacred Drama* — I found myself having to think again about the story of the United Nations operation in the Congo, and to think about it in a new way, partly necessitated by a new theme, and partly by new information. In particular the publication, in 1965, of Miss Catherine Hoskyns's *The Congo Since Independence: January 1960–1961* (Royal Institute of International Affairs, 1965) cast new light on the whole story, especially on the part played by the United Nations in the destruction of Patrice Lumumba.

While I was preoccupied by these questions, I dreamt one night that a new notebook of Dag Hammarskjöld's had been discovered which constituted a sort of political key or equivalent to the spiritual cogitations of Hammarskjöld which have been published under the title *Markings*. In the dream I seemed not to have access to the new notebook, and was vaguely distressed by this.*

Puzzled by this dream, I began, rather reluctantly, to reexamine and reinterpret what I knew or guessed about the fates of Hammarskjöld and of Lumumba. Probably partly by the inherently dramatic nature of these intertwined fates, and partly because of the "sacred drama" thesis on which I was then working, I found it necessary to think in terms of a play. I read *Une Saison au Congo,* by the West Indian poet Aimé Césaire, which is about Lumumba and — to a much smaller extent — about Hammarskjöld. I found it poetically interesting but dramatically and politically unsatisfactory. Césaire's Lumumba I thought too pretty, and Césaire's apparent "acquittal" of Hammarskjöld — who is represented as shocked on seeing how his subordinate has treated Lumumba — too easy a way out. So I had to write my own play.

The germ of *Murderous Angels* is the conception that Hammarskjöld, for exalted and convincing reasons, and in the service of humanity deliberately brings about the downfall and refrains from preventing the death of Patrice Lumumba, which in its turn precipitates his own downfall and death.

In the play, I accept neither the Soviet Government's picture of Hammarskjöld as a sorry lackey of the colonialists nor the immaculate and clear-cut figure which has received so many conventional tributes from Western public men. The record of Hammarskjöld's spiritual and ethical aspirations — in *Markings* — compared with the record of his political course (see Ap-

---

* While working on *United Nations: Sacred Drama* I had read Henry P. van Dusen's *Dag Hammarskjöld: The Statesman and His Faith* (New York and London, 1964) which contains in the form of an Appendix a "Correlation of Dag Hammarskjöld's *Markings* and Facts of His Public and Private Life." The correlation in itself was of little help to me at the time — Dr. van Dusen's approach is reverent, verging on the hagiographical—but the idea of such a correlation seems to have started something.

pendix) requires us, I think, to imagine a different and more interesting person: a gifted, sincere and even exalted idealist who was prepared, if necessary, to act ruthlessly and unscrupulously in pursuit of his ideal, and who found, in the Congo, adequate reasons for believing it necessary to act in this way. This is the figure, and this the situation that I have tried to show in dramatic terms. What is involved, as far as the presentation of Hammarskjöld is concerned, is an imaginative quest for the "missing" political key to *Markings*.

The relations between various episodes in the play and historical events are discussed in the Notes. For the question of Hammarskjöld's death, see the Notes to Act V, Scene II.

II

Murderous Angels is not a "realistic" play, except to the extent that the political conjuncture in which the protagonists are shown as caught was — and in its most ominous implications still is — a real historical situation. The spectacle is of the working of the political fate of human beings: the veiled logic which requires from political men actions which are the function of what they represent — and to a lesser extent of what they are — in circumstances which they cannot ever have wholly foreseen. The movement of this logic, toward the mutual destruction of Dag Hammarskjöld and of Patrice Lumumba, is the movement of *Murderous Angels*. The angels are the great and noble abstractions represented by the protagonists: Peace in the case of Hammarskjöld, Freedom in the case of Lumumba. That the idea of Freedom can be murderous is obvious: this

[xix]

was the angel that both inspired and struck down the hero of Denis Devlin's elegy, from which the concept is taken. To connect Peace with murder seems, on the other hand, shocking, yet the reality of the connection can be demonstrated. The Charter of the United Nations legitimizes the shedding of blood in the defense of Peace. The United Nations peace-keeping operation in the Congo was authorized to use "force if necessary in the last resort," and did so. It is true that the use of force under the sanction of law is strictly speaking not murder. Yet in practice, war includes murder, as the greater includes the less; there can be little doubt that murders, in the ordinary acceptance of the term, did occur in the course of peace-keeping in the Congo, as in the course of all military operations. And the death of Lumumba was certainly murder and no less certainly — as we have seen — a consequence of, among other things, certain decisions taken by United Nations officials in the cause of peace.

It may be said, of course, that those who took these decisions were betraying the cause of Peace, which can never be served by murder, or by actions involving complicity with murder. This seems to me too simple a judgment. Put to yourself a hypothetical case, more extreme than that of Vautrin's Mandarin in *Le Père Goriot*. Suppose you knew a murder to be planned, and suppose that you had the power to avert it. Suppose you also knew, with absolute certainty, that the consequence of averting this murder would be thermonuclear war, the destruction of the world's great cities and of civilization itself, and the creation over most of the world of conditions of anarchy in which, among the survivors of the human race, murder would be a routine occurrence. Would you accept the consequences, and avert the planned murder of a known individual?

Hypothetically, it may not be too hard to give a positive

answer: a good end can never justify bad means, so bang goes the planet. One's answer, if one had to cope with a practical, as distinct from a hypothetical question, might well be different. The questions Hammarskjöld had to answer were practical ones in that they required decisions from him; the consequences of these decisions could only be guessed at. In the shadows of his guesswork was the outline of our hypothetical question. My presentation of how he answered it is, I believe, substantially consistent with what we know of what he actually did. If we condemn what he did, we must at least keep in mind the possibility that we might all be dead if he had acted otherwise. I do not myself think this probable, but there is no doubt that he feared that the Congo might become a Spain or a Korea. This, in turn, could actually have become something worse: a Balkan situation, in which the local commitments of great powers in an unstable region led to world conflict. Only the existence of fears of these dimensions can bring Hammarskjöld's actual decisions into some credible relation to his ethical and spiritual concerns.*

In Sarajevo there stands a monument to Gavril Prinzip, the man who fired the shot that precipitated the First World War. Among his own people, he is remembered not as the torch of the holocaust but as a hero and martyr in the cause of Freedom. Those who rhetorically link the words Peace and Freedom as twin and harmonious ideals should spend some time in meditation before the Prinzip Monument.

---

* There were circumstances which may have tended in the direction of exaggerating such fears. Hammarskjöld's intense desire to build up the United Nations made it natural to lay stress on the enormity of the dangers that the United Nations was averting. Also, an unconscious contempt for an African prime minister may have combined with political pressures into a tendency to see Lumumba "small" against a potentially apocalyptic world background. A novelist might explore refinements; a dramatist has, I think, to use a bolder outline.

For Hammarskjöld, Lumumba was a potential Gavril Prinzip, in the sense of being a threat to Peace; for millions of Africans Lumumba is a Gavril Prinzip, a hero and martyr in the cause of Freedom.

To say that millions of Africans are affected by some event, or impressed by some personality is usually an exaggeration; the continent is vast, its communications poor, the chief pre-occupations of its inhabitants necessarily local. We should not take too literally those orators who tell us that the African masses are awaiting with impatience the decisions of the forthcoming meeting of the Organization for African Unity. But the name and fate of Patrice Lumumba have really reached the minds and hearts of millions of Africans. The thousands of "Café Lumumba" and "Lumumba Chop Bar" signs scattered through countless bush villages in tropical Africa are a more impressive tribute to his memory than the Patrice Lumumba University in Moscow or than that portrait in Stanleyville before which Moïse Tshombe, once his fatal jailer and later for a time his successor as Prime Minister of the Congo, laid one day in 1964 a pious wreath.

In the opposition between Hammarskjöld and Lumumba, it is no accident that the white man is the hero of Peace, the black man the hero of Freedom. *O mors quam amara est memoria tua homini Pacem habenti in substantiis suis!* * Not all white men have peace among their substantial holdings, but the men who do are much more likely to be white than black. For the white man the thought of violent and early death is even more bitter than for the black, because the white man can normally expect to live longer and better. For the white man the thought

---

* What is said here about "blacks" applies generally to non-whites; including, however, the Japanese among the whites, by the well-known South African economic courtesy. "Race" is of course a dramatic expression, exacerbation and freezing of class difference.

of the destruction of civilization is far more terrible than for the black man. It is the white man's civilization, and black men, with few exceptions, have had little more cause to love it than the Israelites had to cherish the civilizations of Babylon and Egypt. The period in which white civilization achieved its definitive preeminence was also, and by no accident, the period in which the triangular trade — guns, slaves and sugar — flourished between Western Europe, West Africa and the Caribbean. The Age of Shakespeare was also the Age of Sir John Hawkins, whose slaving expeditions Shakespeare's Queen disapproved of but invested in. It has been left to a black historian — Eric Williams, now Prime Minister of Trinidad — to remind us, in *Capitalism and Slavery,* of the enormous contribution which the trade made to the formation of capital and to the growth of our civilization. The modern white man of good feeling regrets all this in retrospect; the black man of Lumumba's stamp remembers that it is none the less on this regrettable but lucrative foundation that the character of the modern white man — including such good feeling as he may now afford to indulge — historically rests. Gladstone was the great voice of white liberalism. The family fortune, on which his career was founded, was in its time founded on the slave trade. The family crest, drawn by his father, was a Negro's head shedding drops of blood.*

It is true that black intellectuals, like Lumumba, are necessarily to a great extent intellectual products of white civilization, themselves among the minor legatees of slavery. But it is for the black man an ambiguous heritage; there is a classical process of claiming it, finding it elusive and seeking to reject it. Lumumba, like Ferhat Abbas and Frantz Fanon, went through this; his book *Congo My Country* (1957) expresses

* Sir Philip Magnus, *Gladstone* (New York, 1954), p. 3.

the demand of the acculturated blacks, the évolués, for the same rights as whites, admission to the club. Within a few years he was demanding black power, and a few months later he was dead, murdered by the white man's black servants, those who accepted the status which he had finally rejected.

For those who loved him, followed him and mourned him, Lumumba represented the rejection of slavery, the assertion of human dignity, Freedom. There were white men who saw him precisely in the same light, and therefore worked for his destruction, without any complications of feeling; these are represented in the play by Baron d'Auge and his associates. Theirs is essentially the psychology of the slaver, and the realities of a slave economy are very close to them. The Congo of Leopold II, in which the foundation of the fortunes of such men was laid, was in theory a humanitarian enterprise dedicated to the suppression of slavery.* In fact, it drove the Arabs out of the slave business in order to institute its own system of intensive forced labor yielding large and quick profits at a very high but entirely acceptable cost in black lives. The heyday of this regime ended in 1908, as a result of the revelations of E. D. Morel and Roger Casement. The relatively squeamish public of the period before the First World War was repelled by such details as the system of accounting for expended cartridges by vouchers in the shape of severed human hands, and the outcry on this score led to the transfer of the Congo from the control of the King personally to that of the Belgian state. But the King reserved the rights of that class of people whom he described as "the benefactors of the Congo." These were the entrepreneurs who had been associated with the King in the opening up of the Congo and in the early phases of the exploitation of its human and other re-

---

* For Leopold II see Neal Ascherson's excellent biography, *The King Incorporated* (London, 1963).

sources. Belgium accepted the King's reservation, and the great financial consortia preserved a privileged position and an autonomy almost amounting to sovereignty throughout the whole period of the Belgian Congo (1908–1960). During the period of the action of the play — that is after the Congo had acceded to a nominal independence — these interests were seeking to preserve this autonomy of theirs, by political and military means, especially in relation to the most profitable part of the country, the mineral-rich province of Katanga. They had abjured the cruder practices of the Leopoldine system, while upholding its essential business values, and never ceasing to honor their founder, both in public and in private. Toward the blacks their attitude was, as they said themselves, paternalist; it was a term that did not imply affection, but did imply discipline, condescension, and an interest in hygiene. The company towns of these consortia were comparable to slave ships run on modern lines, with an enlightened slave owner's positive concern for the health and productivity of his stock. White visitors were moved by the evidence of this concern just as some white historians of the slave trade have been moved by the kindness of slavers who had their stock vaccinated against smallpox.* The counterpart of an explicit white paternalism was an implied black *infantilism:* the concept that blacks were a retarded variety of the species, incapable of adult freedom. Lumumba, in rejecting this concept, became in paternalist eyes the equivalent of the leader of a revolt of slaves, which was also a revolt against reality.

Hammarskjöld, obviously, did not share the outlook of the paternalist entrepreneurs. He was a Christian liberal who welcomed what was called the accession of new nations to free-

---

* See G. Freeman-Grenville, *The French on Kilwa Island* (Oxford, 1965).

dom, or — perhaps more precisely — the symbolic extension of freedom which was involved in the access of governments of new states to the attributes of sovereignty. But Peace, not Freedom, was his primary concern, and calculations about world peace had necessarily to be mainly about the positions of those who could make world war. He might deeply disapprove of people like Baron d'Auge, but he had to take account of the power of their alliances in Western Europe and the United States. Lumumba's idea of Freedom, his insistence on "black power now" in Katanga, as elsewhere in the Congo, menaced the delicate mechanism of Peace, and Hammarskjöld's August 1960 flight to Elisabethville symbolized the subordination of Freedom to Peace.

From Hammarskjöld's point of view this seemed a legitimate subordination of the part to the whole; the subordination of the demands of a particular set of people to the universal and overriding requirement of world peace. From Lumumba's point of view it was yet another example of the continued subordination of black to white. The calculations of the political conjuncture were white calculations and Peace — if it were to be Peace without Freedom — was a white vested interest. Lumumba's summoning of Russian aid is a defiant inversion of Hammarskjöld's values; he is willing to risk general war for the sake of his concept of Freedom, expressed in the sovereignty of a black state.* This is not allowed; the black man is not really

---

* This continues to be the position of black revolutionaries. Robert F. Williams, who advocates the use of "the match and gasoline" in American cities, makes a classical statement of the "Freedom before Peace" position: "Four hundred years of violent deprivation can be transformed into an indomitable fighting spirit that may burst forth on the American scene with an intensity more fierce than a hundred hydrogen bombs. The black man will have nothing to lose but his chains, while America has its very existence at stake. For it is better to live just 30 seconds in the glory of human dignity and freedom than to live a thousand years crawling in terror beneath the brutal foot that savagely maintains the tyrant's yoke

free, his state not really sovereign; these things have been pretenses to indulge and flatter him. By testing the sovereignty of his state he exposes its unreality, and destroys himself; Hammarskjöld must side with reality — and therefore against Lumumba — since Peace can only be preserved by taking account of the realities of power.

Lumumba is destroyed, but like Samson he brings down his enemies with him. The flash of his destruction, in its very exposure of the unrealities of the new sovereignties, and in its intolerable light on white power in Africa, creates a new reality, to which in turn the protector of Peace must respond. The martyr of Elisabethville becomes an African demigod, the effort to appease whose devotees will bring Hammarskjöld to his death.

In the end none of them wins because there is no end as yet. Peace is not safe, Africa is not free and even Baron d'Auge, after the collapse of his Katanga, has lost a good part of his investment. The United States, for the time, appears the universal legatee; predominant in the councils of the United Nations, and having its protégé, Joseph Mobutu, in control of all the Congo, including Katanga. Yet these are not secure inheritances. The spirit of Lumumba, the fires of Black Power, burn inside the United States itself.* The mightiest of white societies pours out its resources in vain against one of the smaller of the Asian peoples. A people which sincerely believes it is upholding in

of tyranny" (The *Crusader Newsletter*, Vol. 9 No. 2, October 1967; printed in China). In exactly the same tradition Patrick Ford, in the *Irish World* in the 1880's, used to advocate the setting of London on fire by fifty determined Irishmen "on a windy night." The *Irish World* was printed in New York. Ford drew his readers from those who at the time were contemptuously called the "black Irish."

* "The Report of the Select Commission on Civil Disorder appointed by the Governor of New Jersey acknowledges that the issue of "the place of the Negro in American society" now poses "a clear and present danger to the very existence of our cities." (*New York Times*, 11 February 1968).

the world both Peace and Freedom, finds itself at war with people whose freedom it believes it is defending, but who persist in rejecting the definition of freedom which has to be imposed on them. And those who a few years ago worked for nuclear disarmament, and took part in racially mixed civil rights agitation, now hear from their former black comrades the mocking and ominous cry: *Burn, baby, burn!*

Just as in the play Hammarskjöld and Lumumba do not meet,* so in our world white liberal and black revolutionary have ceased to meet. I do not wish to imply that if the symbolic Hammarskjöld and the symbolic Lumumba could meet, all would be well; it is not at all probable that all will be well. Yet the particular way in which Hammarskjöld and Lumumba did not meet has a continuing significance. The white political leader chooses to bypass the political leader of the blacks, in order to arrange matters with a black man who has been chosen by whites (Tshombe). When the political leader of the blacks rejects these arrangements he is destroyed. This has been the classical choreography of black-and-white relations, since the old frankness of the master-and-slave relation has been abandoned.† The musical accompaniment from the "white" press has sought to convey the feeling that the "black" chosen by the whites is somehow more truly representative of the blacks than is the actual leader of the blacks. It is an increasingly dangerous little dance; in Vietnam, Mr. Johnson's

---

* Historically they did meet during Lumumba's visit to New York (24 July 1960); they did not, however, meet during Hammarskjöld's visit to the Congo. Hammarskjöld on his way out to Elisabethville did not wish to see Lumumba — and Lumumba did not wish to see Hammarskjöld after his return from Elisabethville.

† In the Congo, where the "old frankness" was always rather near the surface, the idea that a black man could be an interlocutor at all was a novelty. *"Amène ton blanc,"* a white man would say to a strange black — "fetch your white man." This form of interracial dialogue continued even after independence.

Tshombe requires already more than 500,000 American troops to maintain him in his position as representative of the Vietnamese people. The freedom of the Vietnamese which the Americans pay so heavily to defend is the freedom of the Vietnamese to have their government chosen for them by the Americans.

Hammarskjöld's flight to Elisabethville, with which the action of *Murderous Angels* begins, is his entry into this *danse macabre*. He enters hesitantly, not accepting Tshombe at his face value, but reckoning with the powerful forces which Tshombe represents, and coming to terms with them for the sake of Peace. In the short run — and he has to deal with short runs — he may be right; the question is left open. None the less it is a tragic choice: "bad magic," as the characters see it. When the white man determines black destinies by talking to another white man in a black mask* the angels rend one another and also rend the protagonists, in turn. This particular dance is always a dance of death for someone, and often for many. If the greatest of white powers insists on continuing to stage it, it may, in a grim and final sense, bring down the house.

Starting from a preoccupation with a particular political conjuncture, and particular human fates in that conjuncture, it would theoretically have been possible for the playwright to transpose all of this into some other country, and some other time. Mr. John Arden successfully did precisely this — in his *Armstrong's Last Goodnight* — with some of the experiences narrated in my own *To Katanga and Back*. Obviously this can be a very good way of writing plays, no doubt in part because the process of transposition is necessarily also one of trans-

---

* "White man in a black mask" may be a black man who has "internalized" white attitudes. Alternatively the black man may be the bought mask of the white man. There are intermediate cases; I believe Tshombe was one.

formation and of creative liberation. Transformation was, however, in this case exactly what I did not want. In the domain of the political the "shock of recognition" does not survive transposition and transplantation, and what I wanted to write was a political play. The minor ruse of changing names — the conflict of Mr. Mulumba and Mr. Sicklebuckler, say — struck me as a pointless and purely nominal evasion. Obviously the dramatic presentation of "real people" would have its dangers too. Yet they are not, and cannot be, "real people": they are imagined characters, with the names and some of the attributes of real historical figures, placed in a dramatic situation matched as closely as possible to the historical situation of those figures.

In the imitation of a historical action, the giving of real names connected with that action to characters who are not real but shaped by the imitation of the action is a proceeding that has the sanction of Aristotle:

"Tragedy is an imitation, not of man but of an action and of life, and life consists in action, and its end is a mode of action, not a quality . . . Tragedy is an imitation of an action, and of the agents mainly with a view to the action . . . But tragedians still keep to real names, the reason being that what is possible is credible; what has not happened we do not at once feel sure to be possible; but what has happened is manifestly possible; otherwise it would not have happened . . . It clearly follows that the poet or 'maker' should be the maker of plots rather than of verses; since he is a poet because he imitates and what he imitates are actions. And even if he chances to take a historical subject, he is none the less a poet; for there is no reason why some events that have actually happened should not conform to the law of the probable and possible, and in virtue of that quality in them he is their poet or maker." [*]

[*] *Poetics* VI, IX (tr. Butcher).

My Hammarskjöld and my Lumumba, then, are not to be thought of as the "real" characters of that name but as personages shaped by the imitation of a real action associated with their names. Their wholly fictitious companions, Diallo Diop and Rose Rose, were shaped in the same way, but at a further remove. They came as confidants to the heroes and took on an existence of their own. The two interracial pairs seem to represent — not through any conscious intent on the author's part — the possibility of a happier relation between black and white than is represented by the Hammarskjöld-Lumumba conflict or the Hammarskjöld-Tshombe collusion.* And it is in the nature of the historical action imitated that these potentially happier relationships should be destroyed.

The Hammarskjöld of *Murderous Angels* is shown as having homosexual tendencies, which are the subject of comment by other characters. The Hammarskjöld of real life was a bachelor whose few close friendships were with men and who was rather generally reputed, inside and outside the United Nations, to be a homosexual: some of his enemies have leveled this "accusation" against him, and some of his friends have judged it necessary to "clear his name" by finding that his affections were "sublimated" to an unusual degree.† The question is not of primary interest in relation to the role of Hammarskjöld in a political play, but I found that I could not convincingly represent him as anything other than a person of homosexual tendencies discreetly expressed. A heterosexual Hammarskjöld

---

* Not to mention the sinister friendship of Munongo and Colonel Zbyre.
† For hostile references to this aspect of his reputation see Trinquier, Duchemin and Bailly, *Notre Guerre au Katanga* (Paris, 1963). For a "defense" see Henry P. van Dusen. *Dag Hammarskjöld: The Statesman and His Faith.* A note at the end of that book contains excerpts from a letter to the author from a Swedish judge who knew Hammarskjöld and refuses to credit the "rumors of homosexuality."

seemed quite impossible and the entirely sublimated creature posited by the hagiographers would be in danger of floating out of the theater altogether.

The presentation on the stage of a discreetly homosexual Hammarskjöld will, I am told, cause pain to those who venerate him as a saint and hero. I hope that any who may be pained in this way may also have their comprehensions stimulated to the point of allowing for the possibility that a man may be a saint and hero and a homosexual as well. When Roger Casement was sentenced to death for treason in 1916, a number of respected persons were prepared to sign a petition in favor of his being pardoned. When, however, documents were circulated to show that he was a practicing homosexual, these respected persons withdrew their names from the petition for a pardon. Their position, apparently, was that homosexuals deserve to be hanged for treason. This is not a state of mind which should be either encouraged or appeased, even in its marginal forms.

I knew Hammarskjöld slightly, but the Hammarskjöld of the play is only distantly related to the Hammarskjöld I knew. Hammarskjöld in the play often speaks of God and of his own mission, rather as the real Hammarskjöld wrote in *Markings*. I never heard Hammarskjöld talk in this way, but it is quite clear that this was his habit of thought, and the presentation of this was essential to the "imitation of the action" which I undertook. Here and elsewhere the dialogue is nonrealistic.

The Lumumba of *Murderous Angels* is in part based on the picture of the historic Lumumba in Serge Michel's *Uhuru Lumumba* (Paris, 1962). Mr. Michel was press attaché to Prime Minister Lumumba: his picture of Lumumba is sympathetic, but — if "but" it be — reveals Lumumba's rather chaotic style of living and leading. The love affair is entirely imaginary but not, I think, wildly out of character* or without its bearing on the action imitated.

I also knew Mr. Moïse Tshombe and Mr. Godefroid Munongo, and in my presentation of these personalities I discovered that my memory sometimes forced me to lapse into realism. These presentations will be found consistent with my account of them in *To Katanga and Back*. For the intervention of the British Consul see also *To Katanga and Back*.†

The presentation of the King of the Belgians as a decent and God-fearing but somewhat limited young man is based on public repute and on a reading of some of the King's speeches.

Ex-President Kasavubu and Colonel (now General) Mobutu are introduced merely to act out — in a somewhat stylized way — the roles which were theirs historically on the occasions represented; many of their lines are the words which they are recorded as having pronounced on these occasions. (See Notes.)

The role of Mr. Rajat Asdal in the play is related to the historic role of Mr. Rajeshwar Dayal of India who took over as Special Representative of the Secretary-General in the Congo, immediately after the events which brought about Lumumba's downfall. Mr. Dayal, for whose high qualities I have expressed my admiration elsewhere, did his best to save Lumumba's life. Asdal's role in the play is a reflection of this effort, but the character should not be taken as representing Mr. Dayal per-

---

* He is on record as approving of interracial alliances: "Q.: Are marriages allowed between Blacks and Whites in the Congo? LUMUMBA: I think that love knows no frontiers" (at the Tribune of the Amis de Présence Africaine in Brussels, 6 February 1960; in *La Pensée Politique de Patrice Lumumba*).

† My once "controversial" account of these curious consular acts seems now to be accepted by historians; see Hoskyns, *op. cit.*, pp. 409–411, 420.

[xxxiii]

sonally, except in the sense that the "imitation of a humane attempt — even though it failed — implies the existence of a humane personality."

With the partial exception of Asdal, none of the characters who do not have "real" names is modeled on a real person. Baron d'Auge and his collaborators represent real forces — as of course do the "faceless" U.N. representatives in Act II, Scene III — but do so outside any realistic convention. Auge began to take shape as a figure who would express, with lucidity and a certain candor, the motivations and political and other calculations of a financier defending his claim to the resources of the Congo in the circumstances of 1960–1961. In doing so he took on a life of his own quite distinct from that of a real financier, who would not be likely, in his discourse on such subjects, so to combine lucidity and candor. If he did, he would have to be rather like Auge, and that would frighten people and be bad for business. So Auge becomes atypical, with a touch of the aristocrat overplaying the businessman, the suppressed romantic overplaying the realist, the renegade ascetic tormenting the pious and conventional with the vision of an irredeemable world.

Chesterton, in *The Man Who Was Thursday*, has an anarchist who, in the course of impersonating a bishop, thinks it appropriate to cry out, on entering a drawing room, "Down! down presumptuous human reason!" The anarchist's bishop, though lacking in representational realism, did express an idea cherished, in a vaguer and more muffled way, by many bishops of the time. He was therefore, in a sense, more true to life than his "models." So may it be with Auge.

The actual representatives in the real modern world, of the forces of which I have made Auge the spokesman, are generally, though not always, so drab that there is little danger that

[xxxiv]

any personage perceptible on a stage can be mistaken for one of them. In the case of Colonel Alcibiade Zbyre on the other hand, the difficulty is that the originals — the French officers of the far right who came to Katanga from Algeria as instructors and commanders of mercenaries and as politico-military advisers in 1960–1961 — were so flamboyant and bizarre that the more fantastic the character which the playwright presents and the more he pushes to the confines of parody and caricature, the more likely he is to hit someone off to the life. This at any rate has not been my intention. No single French officer, fascist, torturer, kidnapper, or murderer has served as the original of Colonel Zbyre.

Monsignor Polycarpe is intended to typify the Europeans of Katanga collectively — including the clergy — in their relation to the powers that then were. A certain clownishness which developed in his demeanor was not intended, but was accepted; it was in fact an element not lacking at the time and place in question, and not without its influence on the march of events.

Mr. James Bonham comes from the area of "area studies": an area which itself deserves to be studied. Here are the shadowy confines where the official world, the business world and the world of scholarship meet. Here a scholar can convert his knowledge of a people or a region into utility to a state or a company, and through this utility win his way into a world of action whose requirements in turn will be likely to influence his scholarly production. Some resist such pressures; some are hardly conscious of them; others become intoxicated by very small sips of power, and some take a romantic pleasure in wearing the voluminous cloak and diminutive dagger of the academic mercenary. Bonham is both nastier and more intelligent than most of his class; he is a sort of bad priest, an anthropologist who hates and despises the people among whom he has worked. The ease with which he can pass from the society of Baron d'Auge into the service of the United Nations will not surprise anyone who knows the relevant conditions. Western diplomacy has one door opening into the world of Baron d'Auge and another into the United Nations; an appropriately connected person, of any nationality, has only to go in one door and out the other.*

Senhora Gattablanca represents on the stage the deep admiration which many people at the United Nations had for Hammarskjöld, and the way in which this admiration was shaken by Hammarskjöld's role in the Congo.

Murderous Angels is a play about real action, not about real people; but the action which it imitates should be of concern to real people. Essentially it is about the threat which actual relations between varieties of the human species present to the survival of the species as a whole.

---

* It is even theoretically possible to imagine an appropriately connected person passing through these channels from the United Nations to the service of Baron d'Auge. The key words, however, are "appropriately connected," and it is hard to imagine why a person who was "appropriately connected" in this sense would be in the United Nations' service at all unless, again, for the sake of Baron d'Auge.

Murderous Angels

Cast Of Characters

COLONEL JOSEPH MOBUTU
RAJAT ASDAL, *Officer-in-Charge of the Congo for the United Nations*
MADAME PAULINE LUMUMBA
BAUDOUIN, *King of the Belgians*
COLONEL ALCIBIADE ZBYRE, *specialist in subversive warfare*
BRITISH CONSUL
REPORTER
ROGER GHEYSSELS, *specialist in kidnapping*

Also

A *Servant, a Photographer, a Sergeant-Major, a Sergeant, a Page, an
Usher, Congolese Soldiers, United Nations Soldiers, Congolese
Women*

ACT ONE

ACT ONE

Prologue

On left side of the stage, a round white table with the sign "Société Universelle." On the right, a round black and white table with the sign "United Nations." At left center a cinema screen, at center a triumphal arch with the words "Independence of the Congo, 30 June 1960." The word "Independence" in black letters on a white ground; the words "of the Congo" in white letters on black. At right center a large map of the Congo. At the table left are seated the Duke of Tamworth and Sir Henry Large-White. At the table right, Australian Delegate, Israeli Delegate and Senhora Gattablanca. At the foot of the arch, left, the Baron d'Auge; at the foot of the arch right, James Bonham. Bonham holds a pointer with which, as the curtain rises, he points at the inscription on the arch.

AUGE

It seems a very simple inscription, does it not? And yet what does it mean? I confess I don't know. I suspect that nobody knows, and that we may all be in for some disagreeable surprises . . . By the way, my name is Auge—Agénor, Baron d'Auge, President of the Société Universelle, at your service. The rather stout gentlemen at the table over there, who may or may not be asleep, are my associates in a number of financial, industrial and commercial enterprises, which are not without importance. As most of these are related in some way to the resources of the Congo, you will understand why it is urgently

[7]

necessary for me to try to decipher this curious inscription . . .
That is why we have here my young friend, Mr. James Bonham,
who is holding the pointer. Mr. Bonham is what is called an
Africanist. Not an African — an Africa*nist*. The distinction is
important. What is an Africanist? Another difficult question.
As far as we European businessmen are concerned, an Africanist is a specialist whom we employ in order to get the better
of Africans — and also of Russians, Americans and so on who
are now engaged in deciphering this inscription in their own
ways. No reflections on your scientific integrity, Bonham, of
course. Well, Bonham, what does it mean?

BONHAM

Well, sir, the trouble is, it's already clear it means radically
different things to different people. Listen, for example, to the
King of the Belgians talking in Leopoldville on Independence
Day.

(*Raps with pointer*)

KING

(KING's *face on screen; recorded voice*)

The independence of the Congo is the consummation of
the work conceived by the genius of Leopold II and continued
with perseverance by Belgium . . . In this historic moment
the thoughts of all of us must turn to the pioneers of African
emancipation and towards those who, after them, have made
the Congo what it is today. They deserve at the same time OUR
admiration and YOUR gratitude . . . When Leopold II undertook the great enterprise which finds today its crown, he
presented himself to you not as a conqueror but as a civilizer
. . . It is up to you now, gentlemen, to demonstrate that we
were right to have confidence in you.

[8]

BONHAM

(*Continuing*)

Well, of course, that's perfectly straightforward.

AUGE

Intelligible . . .

BONHAM

It meant an independence that would be purely . . .

AUGE

Nominal.

BONHAM

It meant that the authority of people like yourselves would continue to be . . .

AUGE

Real.

BONHAM

Exerted through the officers of the Army, who were of course . . .

AUGE

White.

BONHAM

And you know what happened then . .

AUGE

Show . . .

[9]

(*Portrait of* LUMUMBA *on screen.*
Drumming is heard faintly off)

BONHAM

Patrice . . .

AUGE

Lumumba . . .

BONHAM

Prime Minister . . .

AUGE

Of the Congo . . .

BONHAM

Replying to the King of the Belgians.

LUMUMBA

(LUMUMBA'S *portrait on screen; recorded voice*)

Congolese men and women, fighters for independence vic-
torious today, I salute you in the name of the Congolese government . . . As for our fate over the eighty years of colonial
rule, our wounds are too fresh and too painful still for us to be
able to drive them from our memory. We knew exhausting
labor, wrung from us for wages which did not provide us with
enough to eat. We knew sneers, insults, blows, which we had
to endure morning, noon and night because we were Negroes.
Who will forget that to a black man one said "tu," not certainly
as to a friend, but because the "vous" of courtesy was reserved
for whites only . . . We knew that the law was never the same
for white and black; for the first it was accommodating, for the
others it was cruel and inhuman . . .

From all that, my friends, we suffered deeply.

But we, whom the votes of your representatives have chosen to direct the destinies of our dear country, we who have suffered in body and heart from colonialist oppression, we tell you out loud . . . from now on all that is finished.

(LUMUMBA's *face still on screen. A few bars of the cha-cha-cha "Vive Patrice Lumumba, Vive Lumumba Patrice"*)

BONHAM

Well, of course, *that* would be independence to be . . . well, independence to be . . .

AUGE

Independent: which of course cannot be allowed.

BONHAM

Lumumba's speech was bad magic, black magic. And there were other ingredients on that day. Look at this.

(*Raps with pointer. Newsreel film of the incident in which King Baudouin's saber is snatched by a Congolese passer-by. This stops at the point where the Congolese holds the saber and is moving away. This remains on screen as still.* BONHAM *touches with his pointer first the King's white face, then his empty scabbard and white hand, next the black face, then the black hand, then the saber*)

BONHAM

You see? Black magic.

AUGE

Black power.

[11]

BONHAM

Yes, the blacks actually thought independence meant black power. So the black soldiers mutinied against the white officers. They beat the officers and raped their wives. So that the Belgians had to intervene, by sending paratroops —

AUGE

Into Elisabethville, Katanga . . .
(BONHAM *points at Elisabethville*)
At my request. To the place where the copper is, the uranium and the cobalt. Our investments. I must confess that my colleagues and myself were so insensitive as to be more concerned about the possible metaphorical rape of these commodities than about the literal acts of rape which were in fact taking place in other parts of the Congo, which presented less interest, from an economic point of view. So Katanga . . .

BONHAM

Became independent. The paratroops landed in Elisabethville on the tenth of July, and on the eleventh of July Moïse Tshombe, in the presence of the Belgian commander . . .
(*Photograph of* TSHOMBE *with the Belgian
commander, Major Weber*)

AUGE

Declared the independence of Katanga. So that within less than a fortnight this picturesque former colony actually obtained *two* kinds of independence —

BONHAM

The independence of the Congo . . .

AUGE

Lumumba's independence. Black power.

BONHAM

And the independence of Katanga . . .

AUGE

The King's independence. White power with a black front. Our power. My power. We hold Katanga. But can we go on holding it? Lumumba holds the capital of the Congo. But can he go on holding it? What do the Africanists say, Mr. Bonham?

BONHAM

Lumumba must get quick results. Specifically, he must get Katanga — and soon. If he does not, the magic of his appeal will begin to wane and he will begin to die.

AUGE

So that we on our part must play for time. So that the magic may wane and he may die. So that that inscription may mean what we want it to mean.

BONHAM

For his part, lacking the power to recover Katanga by himself, he must look for outside aid. He has appealed to the United Nations. They have agreed to send forces.

AUGE

In order to do what?

BONHAM

No one knows. Except, one supposes —

[13]

AUGE

Mr. Hammarskjöld . . . Now everything depends on how Mr. Hammarskjöld will read this very difficult inscription. Will he read it like Lumumba? In that case he will want to expel the Belgian forces, and we are likely to have black power in Katanga. Or will he read it like the King? In that case he will get rid of Lumumba, and we shall have white power — our power, my power — for all the Congo. Or is there some third possibility? It is hard to say. The inscription remains obscure: the Congo is vast and amorphous: the United Nations represents the nebulous about to plunge into the amorphous. The resolutions are ambiguous: the Secretary-General is subtle, oblique and priest-like: Lumumba is violent, unstable and contagious: the international conjuncture dark, complex and inscrutable. What is clear, however, is the existence of certain concrete interests, which my friends and I must seek to defend by all appropriate means available to us in these bizarre circumstances. Mr. Hammarskjöld will have to go to Katanga. And I must be there before him. And my young friend, Mr. Bonham, curiously enough, will actually be *with* him. A man in my position has friends in all sorts of places.

BONHAM

So I join the United Nations — as an adviser on the African mentality.

(*Joins group at table right*)

AUGE

And I consult my friends before departing for Katanga, to defend our common interests.

(*Joins group at table left. The two groups are spotlit alternately as the dialogue develops*)

[14]

BONHAM

The lady facing me is Senhora Gattablanca, a United Nations official.

(SENHORA GATTABLANCA *inclines her head*)

The gentlemen are delegates. On my left, Israel. On my right, Australia.

(*The* DELEGATES *bow to the audience and resume their seats*)

AUGE

I should like to introduce to you my friend the Duke of Tamworth . . .

(TAMWORTH *bows to the audience and resumes his seat*)

AUGE

(Continuing)

I am Belgian. Tamworth is English. His family was enriched by Henry VIII, mine by Leopold II. These differences are of no importance. Our hearts are united because our treasure is in the same place. And the same applies to my friend Sir Henry Large-White.

(LARGE-WHITE *bows and resumes his seat*)

TAMWORTH

Speaking of our treasure . . .

LARGE-WHITE

We should rather like to hold on to it . . .

TAMWORTH

And we should like to have your views on what we have to do . . .

[15]

LARGE-WHITE

To make damn sure of holding on to it. Now this fellow Lumumba . . .

AUGE

Later, Harry, later . . . For the moment, it is rather a question of Hammarskjöld. What will Hammarskjöld do?

(*Spotlight on table right*)

BONHAM

What will Hammarskjöld do?

ISRAELI

The question is rather: What *can* Hammarskjöld do? In diplomacy the limits of choice are in fact very narrow. In this case they may be too narrow for a man to get through at all.

SRA. GATTABLANCA

You may be wrong. There are things that work in his favor. Afro-Asian support . . .

AUSTRALIAN

The bloody Mau-Mau . . . Sorry, Carmen. Forgetting where I was for the moment. What I meant was that it's all very fine to be loved by the underdeveloped, the underprivileged or — what's the latest one? — the *less technically oriented.* So in Guinea and Mali they all love Dag. So what?

SRA. GATTABLANCA

He is the great diplomat of the cold war. His influence among the Afro-Asians gives him influence with the superpowers. And vice versa. He has the ability, the astuteness, the patience, the

authority of a Talleyrand. But there is a difference. He uses
these great gifts as no other diplomat has ever used them before
— selflessly, in the cause of peace, in the service of Christ . . .

 AUSTRALIAN
(*Glumly*)

Christ . . .

ISRAELI
(*Gently*)

You're right about his ability, Carmen, and I'll grant you
sanctity too, just to please you. And it's true that his popularity
in Afro-Asia gives him some leverage in America at any rate.
But he has come to the fork of the roads. It is in Katanga that
the road forks . . .

BONHAM

How?

ISRAELI

He either gets the Belgians out quickly, or he temporizes. If
he temporizes, his influence with Afro-Asians will decline, and
therefore his usefulness to America will decline. But if he really
starts getting the Belgians out . . .
(*Spotlight on table left*)

TAMWORTH

We should have a thing or two to say about that, I should
have thought.

LARGE-WHITE

Britain is not altogether a spent force, you know . . .

[17]

AUGE

Or if she is, she has been remarkably successful, up to this date, in concealing the fact . . .

TAMWORTH

We are, in any case, not without friends.

LARGE-WHITE

In Parliament. In the Government . . .

AUGE

In the Congress of the United States. In the State Department. Among the owners of newspapers and magazines. And therefore among those who write . . .

TAMWORTH

For newspapers . . .

LARGE-WHITE

And magazines . . .

AUGE

And other media.

TAMWORTH

Money . . .

LARGE-WHITE

Talks.

AUGE

As a conversationalist, money is absolutely enthralling. We make friends in all sorts of odd places. In the academic com-

[18]

munity, for example, which always impresses people for some reason . . . I wonder why that is, by the way? Probably a vestige of the old popular idea that associates learning with holiness. Useful in any case, like the other superstitions of the poor . . . So I think we can say that we have friends everywhere. We have friends in Africa — Tshombe is not the only one who likes our conversation. Why we even have friends in the service of the United Nations itself . . .

(*He waves at* BONHAM, *who waves back as the spotlight shifts*)

ISRAELI

So they can hit him hard, from a great many angles at the same time, *if* they choose to do so. And they will choose, unless he lets down his Afro-Asian friends. Which on the whole is what I think he will do. But if he does that, what is he? What has become of the saint? What has become of the hero?

SRA. GATTABLANCA

(*Agitated*)

That is how it looks. We see it that way because we are not saints and heroes. But he is a saint and a hero. *He is!* And because he is he can transform the situation. Out of what seems to be a trap he can bring new hope. In the Congo, he will fulfill his mission, which should be ours too: in the words of our Charter: "To save succeeding generations from the scourge of war . . ."

AUSTRALIAN

How? By killing Belgians?

ISRAELI

I know he believes that the road to the City of God lies

through the Congo. But what is he going to do when the road forks, in Katanga?

SRA. GATTABLANCA

You do not want to believe what a great man may do, who is also a good man. Listen! I will leave you to analyze and criticize. I cannot answer you. But I am going to pray for him, and for us all.

(*Exit* SRA. GATTABLANCA. *The two parties leave their tables and take up positions on either side of the foot of the arch, forming the two hemicycles of a chorus*)

1ST HEMICYCLE

For there is neither East nor West, border nor breed nor birth . . .

2ND HEMICYCLE

When two strong men come face to face, though they come from the ends of the earth.

1ST HEMICYCLE

That at least was Mr. Kipling's opinion. Or what he presented as his opinion.

And it was regarded as a rather decent thing to say. In the circumstances of the time.

2ND HEMICYCLE

The two strong men in whom we happen to be interested are of course the Secretary-General of the United Nations,

Mr. Dag Hammarskjöld

and the Prime Minister of the Republic of the Congo (Leopoldville),

Mr. Patrice Lumumba

1ST HEMICYCLE

Are they strong men?

2ND HEMICYCLE

That is what we are about to see. They are reputed so, and we must account them as belonging to the category of princes.

1ST HEMICYCLE

Have they come from the ends of the earth?

2ND HEMICYCLE

One of them certainly has. While the other, one must suppose, is already there . . .

1ST HEMICYCLE

Will they come face to face?

2ND HEMICYCLE

That is certainly the intention, but we rather doubt its fulfillment, since Mr. Lumumba is said to be careless about his appointments, while Mr. Hammarskjöld has the reputation of proceeding by indirection

Towards any given rendezvous.

1ST HEMICYCLE

Is there neither East nor West?

2ND HEMICYCLE

We are under the impression that these points of the compass

[21]

Remain in their accustomed relative positions.

Our heroes, you will see, will be praised or blamed at one time or another

For losing the Congo to the East

Or for saving it for the West.

1ST HEMICYCLE

Is there a border?

2ND HEMICYCLE

Most certainly. In fact there are several.

The border of the Congo is in question, and the border of Katanga. The border of Rhodesia will have something to say at a critical moment.

As also will the border of the other Congo.

Of which the capital is Brazzaville.

1ST HEMICYCLE

Is there breed or birth?

2ND HEMICYCLE

Mr. Lumumba was born and bred.

1ST HEMICYCLE

Black.

2ND HEMICYCLE

Mr. Hammarskjöld was born and bred.

1ST HEMICYCLE

White.

[22]

2ND HEMICYCLE

No one throughout the tragedy . . .

1ST HEMICYCLE

No one throughout the comedy . . .

2ND HEMICYCLE

No one throughout what on the whole it is perhaps more tolerable to regard as a kind of game

Ever loses sight of the color of the pieces, even for a moment.

1ST HEMICYCLE

And now, as always in the opening of the greatest of games . . .

2ND HEMICYCLE

It is for white to move.

(They file under the arch)

Scene One

August 1960. Near Elisabethville, Katanga. Residence of Monsignor Polycarpe. Polycarpe, Baron d'Auge. The noise of African drumming is heard through the open window.

POLYCARPE
(*Glumly*)
It's for you. Do you want it?

AUGE
(*Surprised*)
Want what, your Lordship?

POLYCARPE
The drumming. Colonel von Liechtenstein told them to put it on. It's a spontaneous African welcome. Two francs an hour.

AUGE
Why should they put this on for me? . . . a purely private visit.

POLYCARPE
That's right. A spontaneous welcome for a private visit.
(*Extends his right hand and declaims*)
The Katangese nation, proud of its hard-won independence, extends its grateful homage to its benefactor, and worthy son

of the magnanimous Belgian people, the Baron d'Auge, phi-
lanthropist, nobleman, patriot, faithful son of the Church and
President of the Société Universelle! By the way, *are* you a
faithful son of the Church?

AUGE

Well, I . . .

POLYCARPE

No matter, better be one while you're here. We have had
all the atheists deported. They cause Communism. But that's
not the point. The point is: do you want to go on listening to
this stuff all morning?

AUGE

As your Lordship pleases . . .

POLYCARPE

I have been thirty years in Africa. It nauseates me. Boy!
            (*Enter* SERVANT)
Shut the window.
            (SERVANT *shuts window and exits*)
Well?

AUGE

I think your Lordship is probably aware that the purpose of
my visit is in connection with the proposed journey to Katanga
of Secretary-General Hammarskjöld.

POLYCARPE

Is it true that he is a pederast?

[25]

AUGE

I know nothing of that, your Lordship.

POLYCARPE

It's no concern of mine, of course. He's not one of my flock. But I think I read something to that effect in one of the diocesan papers . . .

AUGE

(*Annoyed*)

Your Lordship, I am aware that some intemperate and unwise things have been said and printed here . . . and even repeated on the radio by some of your Lordship's clergy, certainly without your Lordship's knowledge. Among so many grave, spiritual concerns, your Lordship has probably not had the possibility of interesting himself in the diplomatic conjuncture. It remains very grave. It is still possible that Lumumba and what he represents — and that is essentially atheistic Communism, whatever he may claim — may gain a foothold in Katanga, to the grave prejudice of the spiritual, the moral and the social order. And the economic order. If this is to be averted, Hammarskjöld — whatever our personal opinions of him may be — must be handled with the greatest care, and even with every outward mark of respect. That is why — knowing the immense moral influence which your Lordship exerts in Katanga — I have ventured to approach you in connection with the visit.

POLYCARPE

I will do what I can. You are best placed to judge what is possible. But what does he want done? And what do we want with him? Our metropolitan troops hold Katanga securely, and there is nothing any African can do about it. Why can't we continue quietly about our business, and leave these black-and-white buffoons to bluster, in Leopoldville or New York?

AUGE

I would ask nothing better — if we could only count on the United States for unqualified support. The realities of power, in relation to Africa, are such that a local position resting only on the support of a second- or third-rate power cannot withstand local pressures — always liable to be backed enthusiastically by Russia and China, of course — unless it has the support of the United States. So the essential is, always, to know what degree of support is obtainable from the United States, and on what conditions.

POLYCARPE

Well?

AUGE

They are prepared to give us diplomatic support — in terms of helping to keep Lumumba out — for the present, at any rate. But they will only do so indirectly. They fear that if they show their hand, they will make things easy for the Soviets elsewhere in Africa. So they must proceed cautiously and quietly, never getting altogether out of touch with what they call "African opinion."

POLYCARPE
(*Chuckling*)
Can't *we* supply them with that? It's not very expensive.

AUGE
Our friend Tshombe is not quite enough, I'm afraid. The

[27]

Americans have to be shown something that will impress the African states. This means, in practice, that they choose to work through Hammarskjöld, who is supposed to have the confidence of the people they are interested in.

POLYCARPE

How can they be sure Hammarskjöld will work for them? Have they bought him?

AUGE

No. There is reason to believe that he is not for sale.

POLYCARPE
(*Eagerly*)

Blackmail, then?

AUGE

No, your Lordship; it is necessary to imagine, if one can, a context of political transcendence.

POLYCARPE

Bah! . . . Forgive me, I am sure your language was what the situation required. It is the situation itself that troubles me. I don't understand it and also — like these drums — it somehow nauseates me.

AUGE

I fully understand your Lordship's repugnance. Unfortunately it is necessary for us to understand, as accurately as we can, this puzzling, disconcerting and rather distasteful human being. We have been to some pains about this. Investigation has disclosed, for example, that he keeps a very curious diary . . .

POLYCARPE
(Brightening)

He does?

AUGE

Not quite on the lines one might imagine. It is a sort of spiritual diary. It appears from it that he is in the habit of thinking of himself as a kind of Messiah . . .

POLYCARPE

Good God!

AUGE

Exactly. Or sometimes a sort of Pope. A saint, a king, a hero — I don't quite know, it's all very oblique and rather precious. Crucifixion seems to come into it. Listen to this entry — one out of many . . .

*(*AUGE *reads the stanzas)*

I have watched the others:
Now I am the victim
Strapped fast to the altar
For sacrifice.

Dumb, my naked body
Endures the stoning, dumb
When shut up and the live
Heart is plucked out.

POLYCARPE

How disgusting! But what are the Americans to do with this? Can you use a crucified man to run your errands for you?

[29]

AUGE

Apparently, in a way we can — or they can. It is something they call *programming*. The man has what they call a "built-in compulsion" to *save* things, himself, others, how do I know? What he has to save at present is the Congo. He cannot, of course, save the Congo. You and I, your Lordship, know that. But he wants very badly to save it, he wants to believe that he is saving it, he *will* believe that he is saving it, if he can be given a chance to do so. And it is in the power of the Americans — and not at all in the power of anyone else except them — to create and maintain the conditions in which he can go on believing that he is saving the Congo. They can even provide him with a small, but not quite insignificant area of autonomy within which to cherish his hope, or his illusion. In a way, you know, Monsignor Polycarpe, his relation to America is rather like that of man to God; he has free will, but only under and within the omnipotence of the higher power, and it is in these conditions that he must work out his salvation . . .

POLYCARPE

(*Exasperated*)

My dear Baron, in all matters of politics, I can sit at your feet, but would you mind leaving the theological aspects to me? And tell me something in more concrete terms of what we may expect.

AUGE

Your Lordship will please forgive me. I was carried away by my subject, which I must admit fascinates me. As for the specific or concrete terms, I am afraid these cannot be predicted unless we apprehend the problem as a whole; as it were, generically. Specifically, we say: Hammarskjöld will come to Katanga.

POLYCARPE

Sed non et venisse volet . . . I hope.

AUGE

I share your Lordship's hope. "He will come, but he will not also wish that he had come . . ." Rather pleasant, is it not, Monsignor, to reflect that within a radius of five hundred miles from where we sit, there are probably not another two men who could pertinently quote the Virgilian Sibyl or understand what she meant. Let us hope the Sibyl is big magic — if your Lordship does not mind my referring to *that* aspect of the supernatural.

POLYCARPE

We must believe in magic. It is all around us. And even at magic *we* are better than *they* are.

AUGE

(*Coughs*)

Forgive me, Monsignor. The whole subject of race is steeped in magic, of course, and therefore nearer to your Lordship's domain than to my own. My historical studies, however, relatively superficial though they have alas been, incline me on the whole to feel that it is perhaps unwise to dwell too explicitly on certain advantages which, satisfactory as they are at the moment, may prove to be quite marginal and temporary. Let us leave magic and biology aside for some more leisured hour; and let us, for the moment talk politics . . . Hammarskjöld will come to Katanga. But why will he come? He will come because he wants to come and because we — and our good military friends and our good political friends — permit him to come. But why does he want to come? Because he wants to believe he is saving the Congo and through it the United Nations, and because it is only in this direction that the United States allows him to see any hope of a breakthrough in the desired direction. And why do we permit him to come? Because that is our only hope of obtaining a comfortable degree of United States support for what we represent — the preservation in and through Katanga, of the wholesome basic realities of the old Belgian Congo. In short, the reason why Hammarskjöld is coming here, and the reason why we are about to receive him so amicably both reflect ultimately the same thing: United States policy, which we both know to be capable of destroying either or both of us.

POLYCARPE

But to come here, it will be said, to dictate terms — is it not a victory for him and what he represents?

AUGE

Heaven preserve *our* side, my dear Monsignor, from any such victories as that. He himself does not quite see it as a victory, but as an advance. And so it is: an advance into a morass.

POLYCARPE

How?

AUGE

Ponder the scenario. He comes here, not to talk to *us*, of course, but to negotiate with our good African friends,

Tshombe and Munongo, who have been well taught and who will be well briefed — and who, I may add, do not lack in the one case intelligence and in the other character.

POLYCARPE

Faugh!

AUGE
(*Annoyed*)

I am sorry, your Lordship. I'm afraid I cannot have made myself clear. I shall try to do so now. For us at present it is absolutely necessary to avoid giving the smallest sign of what is now called *racism:* an attitude, I know, in favor among our fathers and not without its own stern integrity, but in the present conjuncture potentially prejudicial to our common interests and indeed (if I may say so) common values. Notice that I refrain altogether in accordance with your so just admonition, from any comment on the Christian aspects of the question . . .

POLYCARPE

Thank you very much!

AUGE

So Hammarskjöld will meet Tshombe and Munongo . . . After some stormy scenes, then, which will be more enjoyable for the African participants than for the Scandinavian one, the State of Katanga, of its sovereign grace, will offer certain concessions. These will be the minimum acceptable *to the United States:* they will not be entirely negligible, but not intolerably generous, either: it is mainly a matter of presentation and decor. But, and this is the main part: we know in advance that the United States will press Hammarskjöld to accept these concessions, while Lumumba and his supporters will furiously repudiate them. I think I know what Hammarskjöld will do then and I think I know what Lumumba will do. And I think I know what will happen to both of them . . .

POLYCARPE

I know what Lumumba will do and what will happen to him. What we need to know now is, what will Hammarskjöld do?

AUGE

What can he do? Since he has come here because the United States wants him to come, can he really refuse terms which the United States will tell him represent a triumph for *his* diplomacy? Can he really quarrel with them about this? Can he insist, against them, that his mission has been a failure, and make this gloomy proposition the basis for a quarrel with the indispensable Power? Surely not. They say he is a masochist —

POLYCARPE
(*Brightening*)
Are there any pictures?

AUGE

I was speaking figuratively, your Lordship, meaning that he regards himself as willing to accept suffering. But he is also a proud man. He will wish to believe those who tell him that his mission is a success, the more so in that he knows that the same people have it in their power to make his mission appear a success, to have it hailed as a success by the press, and even to make it *be* a success. Of a kind. The alternative is uninviting and unpromising. We can also show him reasons of a local and picturesque kind for believing what he wants to believe. It will

be important, your Lordship, that he be reminded that the
State of Katanga has deep African roots.

POLYCARPE

It has?

AUGE

Well, perhaps not roots exactly, but African flowers. Like
Moïse and Godefroid. That pair of blooms will be on show of
course. But we must also have plenty of dancing, drumming,
spears —

POLYCARPE

Drumming?

AUGE

I'm sorry, your Lordship. It is as indispensable as it is nause-
ating. From the time of his arrival in your charming diocese,
Hammarskjöld must never have the noise of the drums out of
his ears. Nothing could be more conducive to our purposes:
to help him convince himself that he has truly African and
somewhat mysterious reasons for reaching the quite mundane
and American decision which he will in any case have to
make. We shall take other precautions: there will also be those
around him who will impress his imagination with the inscru-
tably indigenous character of our local institutions.

POLYCARPE

He is a fool then too, this Hammarskjöld?

AUGE

Not at all, your Lordship. He is very clever and very culti-

[35]

vated. If at the moment he may appear rather less clever than someone of much more modest natural attainments, in the person of your humble servant, there is a reason for this. It is that I accept the world as it is, and my own part in it — which is not that of a hero, and cannot be if I am to play it long in this world. Hammarskjöld, on the other hand, wants to play the part of a hero, which has to be a leading part, in this same world I live in, which is a world that does not concede the leading parts to heroes. Or not for long. To play the part as long as he has done, Hammarskjöld has been constrained, by the nature of this world, often to be in fact rather less than a hero: to accept compromises of a kind which moralizers call sordid. His pride, his conception of himself, cannot accept this: as a result he acquires an unusually high propensity for illusion. Thus our little deceptions here are necessary to him: are even a sort of kindness. He is playing a part in our scenario: but we too play a necessary part in his internal one: or rather not us but again our play, or us at work in his play. You see, my dear Monsignor, he is an inverted Don Quixote . . .

POLYCARPE

Inverted? Just as I thought . . .

AUGE

No, no, your Lordship, that is *never* the point. The point is he plays Don Quixote in conditions which often require him to be Sancho Panza. Look! He has come to this castle in the heart of Africa to confront the masters of its mines. If there are giants in the modern world then surely those of us who are masters of its resources and technology are those giants. We are powerful, we are almost incomprehensibly large, we are cruel when we have to be; we are not always bound, your Lordship, by, shall I

say, the more simplified forms of the morality which is taught
in your schools. In short, we are giants such as those against
whom the Quixote of Cervantes thought he was tilting. But
this modern Quixote knows that he must *not* tilt, or this
Rosinante of his will throw him. So his conception of himself
requires him not to see us here. The old Quixote mistook windmills for giants. The new one must mistake real giants for harm-
less windmills, so that he may not have to tilt. And since he
must, let us supply the necessary props: the black windmills.

POLYCARPE

My dear Baron, all this is too hard for me, a simple country
priest. But what you want us to do, I suppose, is to get our
poor blacks to put on some kind of circus: to pretend that this
is their state, so that this Secretary-General of yours may pretend to be taken in, so that the Americans may pretend to believe him, so that finally we may have a chance of being left
in peace to run our own affairs?

AUGE

What a masterly gift for compression, my dear Monsignor!
And what spiritual insight!
(POLYCARPE *rings a bell*)
(*Enter* FATHER BONIFACE, *an African priest*)

BONIFACE

Your Lordship?

POLYCARPE

Get Tshombe for me. Tell him to be here in one hour's time.
(*To* AUGE)
Meanwhile I'm going to take a good look at my begonias.

[37]

There's one thing to be said for this place — you *can* keep a European garden. It's the altitude, you know.

(*Rises, then to* BONIFACE)

Well, what are you waiting for, my boy?

BONIFACE

(*Timidly*)

It is *President* Tshombe whom your Lordship wishes to see?

POLYCARPE

(*Annoyed*)

Yes, Father. *President* Tshombe. Tshombe the holder of the Grand Cordon of Leopold II. Tshombe the two-hundred-fiftieth son-in-law of his Imperial Majesty the Mwata Yamvo. Tshombe the errand boy of the political branch of the Société Universelle. Tshombe whose proprietor, Baron d'Auge himself, is here before you. Baron d'Auge wishes to inspect, at precisely four o'clock, that portion of his property that is represented by Tshombe, Moïse, first President of the Independent State of Katanga, by the grace of Baron d'Auge. See that Tshombe presents himself, properly dressed and sober.

(*To* AUGE)

I suggest that you take a little siesta, Baron, before you see this fellow. He is a whiner and an intriguer like the rest of them, but a little more cunning, and therefore more tiring —

(AUGE *comes forward and takes* BONIFACE's *hand, to the obvious surprise of the priest and* POLYCARPE)

AUGE

Father, it is true that I am Baron d'Auge, that I would like to see President Tshombe, and that the interview would perhaps best be held here, to avoid exciting unnecessary remark.

[38]

For the rest, you certainly know his Lordship's sense of humor far too well to take seriously the delightful tirade he has just delivered, in the best prose style of our reckless and unscrupulous adversaries . . .

BONIFACE

Yes, my lord.

POLYCARPE

Of course, Baron, of course . . . I am just an old priest, a very simple old priest, who is going to take a turn in his garden . . .
    (*Exit* POLYCARPE. BONIFACE *is about to leave in his wake, but* AUGE *stops him*)

AUGE
(*Softly*)
Father Boniface . . . I should like just a moment of your time . . . May I ask . . . are you a Katangese?

BONIFACE
(*Under the stress of some strong emotion near to tears*)
A *what?*

AUGE
I asked what you were, Father Boniface . . .

BONIFACE
I am a priest . . . an African priest.

AUGE
And of what nationality?

[39]

BONIFACE

Congolese.

AUGE

Indeed — *Congolese* not *Katangese?*
(*A pause*)

BONIFACE

I know nothing of politics, my lord. Before, they told us we
were Congolese. Now they tell us we are Katangese. I have
embraced a life of obedience, my lord, but I am a man and
sometimes I forget.

AUGE
(*Very softly*)
So then, Father, when you remember . . . you are now a
Katangese, are you not?

BONIFACE

Yes, my lord.

AUGE

And so, M. Moïse Tshombe is your President, is he not?

BONIFACE

Yes, my lord.

AUGE

And do you respect your President?
(*Silence*)
You should respect him, shouldn't you? As a Christian? A
true Christian?

BONIFACE

(*Breaking out at last*)

How can I respect him when I see that you do not respect him? When his lordship makes a joke of him? Whether white people laugh openly, as he does, or keep a straight face, as you do, it is all the same. Tshombe is still your black servant whom you have dressed up like a President. Whatever Tshombe says, what he means is always what you mean and what you mean — whatever you say — is always that we continue to be your slaves.

(*Manages to control himself, breathing heavily*)

AUGE

(*In a friendly tone*)

Thank you, Father, for your frankness. It is refreshing and illuminating — like a fountain. One word more.

BONIFACE

Yes, Baron d'Auge?

AUGE

Do you respect Patrice Lumumba?

BONIFACE

They tell us that he is a Communist . . .

AUGE

Quite . . . But do you respect him?

BONIFACE

If he is a Communist, and *if* all they tell us about Communists is true, I could not respect him.

[41]

AUGE

So that if what they told you, or some of what they told you, were not true, then . . .

BONIFACE

(*Defiantly*)

I *do* respect him. And I already know that many things they tell me are not true, and that they do not believe them themselves.

AUGE

(*Laughing*)

Monsignor Polycarpe has already counseled me not to meddle with theology! In any case, it is your opinion of Lumumba that interests me. Why do you respect him?

BONIFACE

Because he has made *you* respect him.

AUGE

And how do you know that he has made us respect him?

BONIFACE

(*In a low voice*)

Because you hate him so.

POLYCARPE

(*Voice outside*)

Father Boniface! Father Boniface?

AUGE

Thank you, Father Boniface . . . And good luck!

[42]

(*Exit* BONIFACE)
(*Enter* POLYCARPE)

POLYCARPE

Where has that fellow got himself to? I want him to explain
to the gardener . . . The gardener pretends not to understand
my Swahili. He does it out of spite . . . Thirty years in Africa
and still . . .

AUGE
(*Coldly*)

My dear Monsignor, I'm afraid I must interrupt both your
gardening and your reminiscences. Please sit down.

POLYCARPE
(*Shocked at the change of tone*)

Baron! Are you telling me to sit down — in my own residence?

AUGE
(*Crisply*)

Yes, and in a moment you will sit down. Listen, in normal
times I talk to you as if you were a great churchman, and I a
humble layman. Don't let these formulae of courtesy mislead
you as to the facts. The facts are that I am power, and you are
a façade. Because we live in dangerous times, and because you
have behaved indiscreetly, I am forced to remind you of some
facts of life. A word from me and you could be put on the re-
tired list, on health grounds, and confined to a suitable estab-
lishment . . . Or you could be transferred to Stanleyville and
a martyr's crown, which probably would not fit you very well.

If you want to continue in your present comfortable seat, among your begonias, you will sit down when I tell you. Sit down.

(POLYCARPE *sits down*)

You will immediately give a year's leave to that young man Boniface, to take up a scholarship which I will offer him in Belgium. I shall in due course supply in his stead a suitable secretary, white, on whose discretion I can count and whose stipend I will pay.

POLYCARPE

But . . . what if Boniface doesn't want to leave?

AUGE

If he refuses, I shall inform the Head of Security here in Elisabethville that Boniface is a Lumumbist, which he is or will be. What happens then is not my concern. As you know, all known Lumumbists in Katanga are dead.

POLYCARPE

A Lumumbist? Why?

AUGE

Because he wanted to keep his self-respect. And how else, being what he is, could he keep it? Here? With you? But of course self-respect is much too expensive a thing for a man like him to keep. So he must either swallow his pride, under my personal supervision, or he must die.

POLYCARPE

And in the meantime I have no secretary.

AUGE

No, and that is as well. You lack self-control, Polycarpe, and

[44]

you let black men see that you despise them. At present that is
a dangerous luxury which you cannot afford and which I will
not permit you. If we must speak of puppets — a crude term,
but sometimes useful — new, shiny, black puppets are more
valuable these days than battered old dolled-up white ones
like Monsignor Polycarpe of Katanga. So mind your manners,
and don't aspire to a racist arrogance which is now beyond
your means . . . I'm sorry: your Lordship's means.

POLYCARPE
(*Sullenly*)
You can still afford to be a racist, I suppose.

AUGE
(*With dignity*)
You are mistaken. I have never been a racist. I have never
despised black men more than I do white ones.

Scene Two

The following day: afternoon. The Elisabethville airport.
Tshombe, Munongo. Tribal chiefs in their regalia. Drummers
drumming. Dancers dancing. African soldiers in dress uniform.
A uniformed band, which at first is not playing. The only white
people on the stage are the Commentator, who wears a white
cassock, and the Photographer. An aircraft flight of steps down
which enter Hammarskjöld, Diop and Bonham. Tshombe and
Munongo step forward and greet Hammarskjöld. Smiles all
round, except for Munongo. Photographs. Tshombe and
Munongo step back. The uniformed band strikes up with the
drummers. Tshombe and Munongo stand to attention. A very
large Sergeant-Major steps forward holding an enormous flag
(green, white and red with copper crosslets) which he holds
above the group formed by Tshombe, Hammarskjöld, etc. Pho-
tographer very busy and energetic. Everyone at attention, ex-
cept Hammarskjöld and his party who should look embarrassed
but vaguely respectful like agnostics in church. They should
also slump slightly, to show they are not standing at attention.
Soldiers at the salute. Civilians uncovered.

COMMENTATOR

Here is Radio Katanga, Elisabethville, Katanga — Africa's
shield against Communism! Katangese! Our beloved country is
passing through a memorable hour! While I speak, the Secretary-General of the United Nations stands at attention to our

[46]

noble National Anthem. He has just inclined his head in homage to our glorious flag. Already, without a word spoken, he has extended a silent but eloquent recognition to our nationhood. Katangese! Secretary-General Dag Hammarskjöld, a man renowned throughout the world for his wisdom and humanity, has already — discreetly but unmistakably — recognized the justice of our cause! This simple but immensely moving ceremony is the international baptism of our multiracial nation, pledged as it is to eternal friendship between black and white. This ceremony spells death to the agitators, the Communists, the trouble-makers, the so-called Government of the so-called Congo. The man whom they themselves called in to crush us, here silently repudiates them and marks them out for the doom they deserve. Long live Secretary-General Dag Hammarskjöld! Death to Patrice Lumumba!

The crowd takes up the cry. "Vive Hammarskjöld! Mort à Lumumba!" Drumming. As Tshombe, Hammarskjöld and their parties move to exit, Munongo remains behind and holds the center of the stage. Silence. He raises both his arms above his head. The drums begin again. They rise in sound while Munongo lowers his extended left hand to point at the ground, and slowly draws his right arm across his throat. The crowd roars "A Mort! A Mort!" The drums rise in a deafening crescendo.

Scene Three

*A room at the Hotel Leopold II, Elisabethville. A little later
the same afternoon. Drumming is heard from outside throughout. Hammarskjöld, Diop. Diop is sitting at a desk with pencil
and paper, staring in front of him. Hammarskjöld moves across
the room and puts his hand on Diop's shoulder. Diop rises and
walks over to the window, then turns facing Hammarskjöld.*

HAMMARSKJÖLD
(*Puzzled*)
What's the matter, Diallo? Having trouble with the com-
muniqué?

DIOP
Dag . . . Can't you see that no communiqué is ever going
to beat this one?

HAMMARSKJÖLD
But it was you yourself who thought it was so urgent to do
something to undo the effect of those fantastic proceedings at
the airport . . .

DIOP
Yes, to *do* something. Not to write something.

HAMMARSKJÖLD
Words are action. That is the principle of diplomacy. That is

the principle by which I live: the struggle to substitute the play of appropriate words for the mechanisms of violence.

DIOP

What if the principle by which you live is not a principle of life? What if violence is as necessary to life as food and drink?

HAMMARSKJÖLD
(*Gravely*)

Do you think, Diallo, that that possibility has not occurred to me? It is even, in terms of the world of sense, a probability. But I have chosen — or, as I think, I have been chosen — to act as if it were not so. To act as if spirit can work upon brute matter: to act as if the only life worth living were life in the service of the spirit, the unending struggle to impose upon the pattern of events the mark of Christ.
(*Silence*)

DIOP

Yes, Dag, but the pattern resists the mark. You are a soldier of Christ, you are the spiritual hero of our time. That is one of your parts. The other one, for the moment, is that of straight man in a black farce in an African company town. Scenario by courtesy of the Société Universelle. All profits to go to charitable foundations for the preservation of lynching and slavery. The mark of Christ! Christ! . . . Well, at least you've come to the right hotel . . .

HAMMARSKJÖLD
(*Hurt and puzzled*)

The Leopold II? Oh, I see. You mean that, like the King, I'm a hypocrite mouthing sanctimonious phrases to cover odious transactions . . . Diallo, Diallo, do you really believe that?

DIOP

(*Hard*)

What does it matter what the Secretary-General's nigger companion believes or doesn't believe? What matters is what the Secretary-General's going to do now. Are you going to pack your bags and go home, so marking your repudiation of your bit part at the airport? Or are you going for a nice chat with Moïse?

HAMMARSKJÖLD

I'm going for a nice chat with Moïse. Which is what I came here for. And I am going to arrange the modalities for the entry of the United Nations troops into Katanga.

DIOP

We've already seen the most important of the — modalities. Do you realize what they will do with that picture: Tshombe, the flag of Katanga, the Secretary-General . . . Do you realize that every politically conscious black man in the world, every man for whom the word Tshombe means what the word Quisling means to you, will see that picture as the symbol of the great betrayal — as meaning that the white man whom they trusted — yes, and loved — is just like all the other white men. Do you realize that from this day on Lumumba must be your enemy? Do you realize . . . ?

HAMMARSKJÖLD

Realize, real, realist. All words for dragging men down, for denying the possibilities of man and of the spirit. I refuse to

[50]

realize. I try to understand. That means trying to grasp more than the surfaces of things. One *stands under:* under the will of the spirit, under the acceptance of the burden, under the necessary humiliation without which there is no understanding. If you can accept the fact that you are under, and are going under, and yet you can still stand, then you are one of the few that can speak of understanding. Do you think I felt nothing, while I stood before that flag and listened to that anthem? I felt my future narrowing: I was rushing down the contraction of a cone towards that predictable point where it must close on me and crush me. I know that Lumumba and I, henceforward, may be drawn into deadly opposition. The hope of the black men may be drawn for a time to fight against the hope of all mankind.

DIOP

(*Incredulously*)
The hope of all mankind? That is to say, Dag Hammarskjöld?

HAMMARSKJÖLD

The United Nations is the hope of all mankind. That is its meaning, its only meaning. We call it an organization, but it is much more like a prayer. The prayer is there in the opening of the Preamble to the Charter: "To save succeeding generations from the scourge of war, which twice in our lifetime has brought untold sorrow to mankind." But a real prayer is more than a recitation of certain words: it is also an immense spiritual effort. The life of the Secretary-General must be entirely dedicated to that effort. Yet, though it is essentially a spiritual effort, it must go forward in the forms of an entirely secular and profane activity. It is marked with the seal of the will of God. "Thy kingdom come, Thy will be done" . . . But if Thy kingdom has not come, how is Thy will to be done? How is a man to bring peace, or to protect such peace as there is, in a world dominated by greed and cruelty? Are you to refuse to have any commerce with the masters of greed and cruelty and with their servants? Are you to say: "No, I will not be contaminated, I will not compromise, I will not betray!"

DIOP

Well? Are you to say that? The world is waiting to hear.

HAMMARSKJÖLD

No, Diallo. I accept contamination, I accept compromise, I accept betrayal. I accept the betrayal of myself by others, and the betrayal of others by me.

DIOP

But just for the moment it is the others who are to be betrayed. And they happen to be black. Do I guess right?

HAMMARSKJÖLD

Those who have to be sacrificed in the cause of world peace are not of any particular color. Do you remember the Hungarian affair? That was a case of a people struggling to be free: quite as clear a case as that of the Congo, if not more so. They appealed to the United Nations if you recall. The Americans were generally regarded as morally committed to come to their aid. But they wisely decided not to come to their aid, as that would risk general war. That was a sound decision and also a sordid one, since the world is so constructed that the sound decision is often the sordid one. And as it was so sordid, and as none of us can bear the spectacle of how we really are, they needed a compensatory spectacle in which they would appear righteous. They needed to act out in words the part of defending and avenging angel which they had been too prudent to act out in deeds. Now, one of the ways in which the United Nations protects the peace is by providing the most impressive possible theater for a spectacle of this kind: a spectacle which is a ritual and dramatic substitute for war. I stage-managed that spectacle for them. I helped them to save the peace by betraying the Hungarians. And I am prepared if necessary to behave in the same way towards the Congolese.

DIOP

It's funny how often saving the peace and doing what the Americans want turn out to be the same thing . . .

HAMMARSKJÖLD

It's not a coincidence. The Americans are the most powerful nation on earth, and therefore the most dangerous to peace.

(*Enter* JAMES BONHAM. *From the moment of his entry* DIOP *adopts a more formal demeanor*)

BONHAM

I'm sorry to disturb you, sir . . . Hello, Diop . . . There's a call coming through from Leopoldville . . . Ralph Bunche . . . Very urgent and important. Will you take it yourself, sir?

HAMMARSKJÖLD

No, Bonham. I'm not taking any chances with a tapped line. You take the call on this telephone when it comes through. Make no comment of any kind, whatever is said, except that you will report to me.

BONHAM

Yes, sir.

(*Takes up telephone to give instructions for the call*)

DIOP

Secretary-General . . .

HAMMARSKJÖLD

Yes, Diop?

DIOP

There are one or two further points I should like to offer for your consideration, if I may.

HAMMARSKJÖLD

Certainly.

DIOP

If I understood rightly, your main concern here is to prevent the Congo crisis from turning into something like a Korea or a Spain, with both sides in a civil war calling in international support, and increasing the risk of world war.

HAMMARSKJÖLD

Yes, that is why I'm here.

DIOP

I am very much afraid that the risk of a Korea or a Spain is now increased by your remaining here, after what happened at the airport.

HAMMARSKJÖLD

Why?

[54]

DIOP

Radio Katanga has the most powerful transmitter in the Congo. A gift from the Société Universelle. Katanga has also the most efficient publicity service in the Congo: for similar reasons. The broadcasts, the press coverage and the photographs of your arrival here will make up an unbearable humiliation for Prime Minister Lumumba. He will certainly feel that he can no longer rely on the United Nations and that he must look elsewhere. And where can he look? He cannot look to the United States because he knows they fully support your mission here, as do the other Western countries. So he will have to turn to the other superpower. And if the Soviet Union becomes deeply involved, so will the United States, and there you have the raw material for your Spain or your Korea . . .

HAMMARSKJÖLD

I have considered these possibilities . . . But I think you exaggerate. Lumumba will certainly be annoyed, but he will probably come round eventually, and it would be unreasonable of him to go as far as you suggest. We can get out a press release, rejecting the implications of our reception — though that will have to be delicately done . . . And I will see Lumumba immediately on my return.

DIOP

(*Earnestly*)

Sir, if this were not an African matter, I would not challenge your judgment. But I am an African and I know how we react. This is not a land in which words can compensate for gestures and pictures. Hundreds and thousands of people who cannot read your words, hundreds of thousands who could not understand your words, even if they heard them on the radio, since

[55]

they must be "delicate" diplomatic words; these hundreds of thousands of Congolese will see those pictures, and hear and understand what Radio Katanga says. And they will believe the radio, when they see the pictures of you with Tshombe and Tshombe's flag, and they will say: "This white man, who said he was our friend, is Tshombe's friend." And they will say "Patrice, do not trust this white man." And Lumumba, whose strength is his closeness to these ordinary people, Lumumba who essentially feels and thinks in the same way, will react in the way dictated by his own feelings, which match what his people expect of him. He will react not with a carefully measured expression of irritation, as an experienced European politician would, but with a flamboyant gesture, something deliberately excessive, conspicuously outdoing the provocation offered. And there is really only one such gesture open to him: he *must* seek Soviet help . . . With all your experience, Secretary-General, you do not yet know tropical Africa: you have not become familiar with the density of the medium in which you are working. Those who staged the ceremony at the airport just now understood that medium by long experience. That ceremony was meant to be, and is, terribly bad magic both for you and for Lumumba. It works, like all magic, on nerves and minds. The spell will not be broken by a press release or a communiqué. It can only be broken by a gesture, symbolizing refusal. You must return immediately, Secretary-General, without seeing Tshombe, or your mission will end in catastrophe.

(*A pause*)

HAMMARSKJÖLD
(*To himself*)
There are things I had not seen . . .

[56]

(*To* BONHAM)

You'd better ring Tshombe's office. Tell them that I am obliged, by an unexpected turn of events, to return to Leopoldville, without being able to keep my appointment with him. The modalities of my possible return can be discussed with my representative here. That is all that needs to be said officially. In response to their protests you can let it be known that the forms of their reception were such as to prejudice the fruitfulness of any meeting at this time. The same to be leaked to the press, not for attribution. And tell the pilot of the *Anne-Marie* to be ready for an immediate take-off.

BONHAM

Yes, sir. (*Makes no move*) Sir, if I may offer a suggestion . . .

HAMMARSKJÖLD

Certainly.

BONHAM

This call from Leopoldville, sir. It seems to be important. And it may have a bearing on your decision . . .

HAMMARSKJÖLD

Yes . . .

BONHAM

It should be through any minute. I don't think you would lose anything by taking it before we put the message through to Tshombe.

[57]

DIOP
(*Tensely*)

Secretary-General, if I am right, this is the most urgent decision of your life.

HAMMARSKJÖLD
(*Cooly*)

That's not a reason why it should be taken in more ignorance than is absolutely necessary.

BONHAM

One other point, sir. There's a lot in what Diop said just now: I don't deny that at all. But there is another side to it. Tshombe is an African, too. He will lose a tremendous amount of face by your precipitate return. That will make him just as angry as the photos and so on could make Lumumba. Tshombe too will feel the need to compensate by some extravagant gesture which may endanger . . .

(*The telephone rings.* BONHAM *takes up the receiver, makes notes on a pad*)

Dr. Bunche . . . Yes, I can hear you. Very faint, though . . . No, the Secretary-General has asked me to take the call for him . . . Yes, he does know it is you . . . I'm not authorized to make any comments, just to take a message . . . Yes . . .

(*To* HAMMARSKJÖLD)

Lumumba called a press conference, immediately after Radio Katanga had its broadcast about your arrival. They say his statement is very bad. Extremely violent.

(*At receiver again*)

What was that? (*Writing*) "Imperialist lackey," "hypocritical Jesuit," what kind of "jackal"? Oh, "mangy." I see . . . No. If it's all like that, you needn't go on . . . I see . . . I see. No, we can't make any comment from this end . . . Yes, I'll tell the Secretary-General immediately. Thanks. (*Hangs up. To* HAMMARSKJÖLD) Well, that's torn it, sir. Lumumba says he has lost all confidence in you and in the United Nations, and that the Soviet Ambassador has promised him all the aid he needs to throw the Belgians out of Katanga. He added a great deal of extravagant abuse directed at you. Sounds as if he was drunk, actually . . .

DIOP

Not necessarily. These niggers just can't control their feelings, the way civilized people do.

HAMMARSKJÖLD

That doesn't help us much, Diop . . . You were right about his reaction. But his reaction, now it has become public, makes your advice not wrong, but no longer relevant. I cannot now turn back, because I would seem to do so at his command. To turn back in these conditions would lower the prestige and authority of the office of Secretary-General, and so weaken the defenses of peace. The gate has closed behind me, and I must go forward. I do it with the darkest forebodings, but I can do nothing else. The appointment with Tshombe stands.

DIOP

Secretary-General . . .

HAMMARSKJÖLD

I am very sorry, Diop, more sorry than I can say. But the discussion is over; the decision is taken. Now I need some time to think before I meet this man.

[59]

(*Exit* HAMMARSKJÖLD)

BONHAM
(*To* DIOP)

Well, you put up a very good show. I especially liked the "mysterious Africa" bit. (*Mimics*) "You have not become familiar with the density of the medium." Just the right note. And the stuff about ceremony and magic was very well-pitched too. Just the thing to catch the old Scandinavian highbrow witch doctor. In fact you pitched it a bit strong. From the look on his face, I think he half believes that that nonsense at the airport *was* magic, and that he has caught his death from it. God knows what that idea will do to him . . . You nearly talked him out of meeting President Tshombe, nearly changed the course of history . . . But you couldn't quite pull it off, could you? Do you know what the trouble is?

(DIOP *is silent and unresponsive*)

The trouble is you know him too well . . . I don't take any stock — or not much stock — in the usual gossip about our Secretary-General's propensities. The real thing, psychologically, is that he's a narcissist. He's in love with himself, and it's just like any other love affair. If he becomes friendly with someone, then he immediately becomes jealous of that person, for being on too friendly terms with his beloved — to wit, himself. So the relations cool, you see, Diop. The influence wanes, if you take my meaning.

DIOP
(*As if he had barely been listening*)

Tell me, Bonham, is there any scientific basis for the widespread belief that black men are constitutionally less intelligent than white ones?

[60]

BONHAM
(*Reflectively*)

Interesting you should ask me that. We had a seminar on the subject at St. Swynhilde's last term, as a matter of fact. It was financed — this will make you laugh — by the Société Universelle. Inconclusive, of course, but opened up some interesting lines of inquiry. The correct, decent, liberal answer to your question, of course, is to look you straight in the eye and say: "No, Diop, there is no scientific basis for that belief." The fact is, though, that no one really knows whether there is a scientific basis for it or not. We don't know because we haven't really looked — we haven't carried out an inquiry on the scale required, backed by all the resources of modern science. And the reason we haven't looked is that we have been afraid of the political repercussions of what we might find out. Because, you see, there is no obvious reason why there shouldn't be quite sizable differences between the intelligence levels of different varieties of the human species, as there are obvious differences in other characteristics. And if there are differences in intelligence levels, we might expect these to show a positive correlation with differences in historical performance. And you see where we get then, Diop? This would amount to admitting that those disgusting old racists were right. There would be those who would argue, for example, that the most intelligent of the human races has the best right to control and exploit the resources of the planet. Including Africa, of course. And indeed including Africans. An interesting train of thought, don't you think?

DIOP
(*Softly*)

The answer is not in words. It's in blood. The time is coming when men will die because of what you think, and of what I feel about what you think.

BONHAM

Splendid stuff, Diop, splendid stuff. I think meantime we'll all have a nice cup of tea with Mr. Tshombe.

ACT TWO

ACT TWO

Scene One

Two days later. Leopoldville. Residence of the Prime Minister of the Congo, Patrice Lumumba. An office. Lumumba, Madame Rose. The office is in great disorder, Lumumba has bottles, glasses and a drawn sword before him on the table. In a corner on the floor is a portrait of King Baudouin, upside down.

MADAME ROSE
(*Holding a telephone*)
It's Hammarskjöld's office again. Hammarskjöld's plane is due to leave in two hours' time and he insists on seeing you. What are they to tell Hammarskjöld?

LUMUMBA
Tell him to go fuck himself. If he knows how.

MADAME ROSE
(*Smiling, speaking into telephone*)
Yes, Mr. Diop, I have just checked with the Prime Minister. He has reiterated — in quite forceful terms — his conviction that no useful purpose would be served by such an interview. He feels, as you know, that the circumstances of the Secretary-General's visit to Elisabethville are such as to show that the United Nations either cannot or will not accomplish what the Government of the Congo invited it here to do —

that is to say, get the foreign troops out of Katanga, and create the conditions for the reunification of the Congo. The Prime Minister has therefore no further use for the United Nations. He will pursue the national objective by other means. He will not see Mr. Hammarskjöld either now or ever . . . Oh . . . yes . . . I will, but . . . (*To* LUMUMBA) It's Hammarskjöld himself. He absolutely insists on at least talking to you on the telephone. He says it's literally a matter of life and death . . . And he asked me to be sure to repeat those seven words: "Literally a matter of life and death" . . .

LUMUMBA

Very well, tell him to drop dead.

MADAME ROSE
(*Speaking into telephone*)

Would you please hold on for a moment, Mr. Hammarskjöld. I'll try to . . . to reach him. (*To* LUMUMBA) Patrice, I . . . I think you ought to see him . . .

LUMUMBA
(*Gently*)

No, Rose, the answer is no. Still no, and always no.

MADAME ROSE

Patrice, I'm frightened . . . You didn't hear the way he said those words . . . He meant them. He meant *your* life. And, my God, he meant your death . . . Something is going on, Patrice . . .

LUMUMBA

Something is always going on. This is the Congo! C'est le Congo!

(*He hums a tune and begins to dance a cha-cha-cha*)

MADAME ROSE
(*Into the telephone*)
I'm very sorry to keep you, Mr. Hammarskjöld . . . I'm still
trying to reach him . . . I don't know . . . I . . . I hope so,
Mr. Hammarskjöld.

LUMUMBA
(*Stops dancing*)
Oh you "hope so, Mr. Hammarskjöld," do you, Rose? I must
look out . . .

MADAME ROSE
Yes, Patrice, you must look out. You must! You must! Patrice,
my dearest love, you are in terrible danger. I think that if you
do not take up this telephone and talk to this man, they are
going to kill you . . .

LUMUMBA
Who's going to kill me? Hammarskjöld? That fellow couldn't
kill a chicken. (*He imitates a man chasing a chicken, clucks
like a chicken, catches imaginary chicken and chops with his
hand, then in an effeminate screech*) "The blood! The blood!
The sin, the sin!"
(*He falls back in his chair laughing*)

MADAME ROSE
Patrice, my dear, there's very little time . . . For God's sake
protect yourself, Patrice! What Hammarskjöld has to tell you
is about a threat to your life. It's *suicide* not to hear him. You
know there are powerful men who are out for your blood . . .

[67]

LUMUMBA

Blood!

(*He snatches the sword and slams the flat of it on the table*)

If they want blood they can have it! Buckets of it!

(*He knocks over a full bottle of beer, then with a sweep of the sword he sends all the bottles and glasses flying from the table*)

By God, if we're savages, let's *be* savages and have some sport before they kill us off. Kill the white man! Kill the white man! Kill! Kill! Kill!

(*He stamps around the room slashing the air with the sword.* MADAME ROSE *turns her back and speaks into the telephone, then hangs up. As she hangs up,* LUMUMBA *comes up behind her and touches the small of her back with the point of the sword*)

Death to the whites!

(MADAME ROSE *turns around. He holds the sword pointed at her*)

MADAME ROSE
(*In tears, smiling*)

All the whites, Patrice?

LUMUMBA
(*Firmly and calmly*)

All the whites, Rose dear. Every one. (*He sticks the sword into the floor*) Come, let's dance. (*They dance around the sword*) You're not white — you're pink. Pink's all right! A good African color. I once was pink myself — did you know that?

MADAME ROSE

Yes, Patrice. You must have been pink when you were a baby.

LUMUMBA

African babies are pink: it's an ethnological fact. In fact, it's because they're pink that you know they're black. Funny, isn't it? (*She starts crying*) Come on, Rose! Chin up, Rose! We haven't got very long. Let's live it up while we can.
(*He sings*)
I too was pink like you!
Pink like you! Pink like you!
One day! One day!
Be black like me, won't you?
Be black like me, won't you?
Some day! Some day!
It's the least that you might do
Since I was pink like you.

MADAME ROSE
(*Begins to laugh*)
All right, Patrice, I will. You must think of me as a black person in — in immature plumage!

LUMUMBA

(*Laughs delightedly, whirling her round the room, his cheek against hers*)
Soft plumage! Pink plumage! Let's go to bed.

MADAME ROSE

Mr. Prime Minister! You just can't go to bed with your sec-

[69]

retary in the middle of the afternoon, in the middle of a major
crisis . . .

LUMUMBA

In the middle of my secretary! (*Laughs boisterously*) Can't
I just! Rose, you've a lot to learn about Africa before your
plumage turns. Africans are sensible people. They expect their
leader to have a bed, and someone to go to bed with — and if,
when they come to see him, they hear that he's in bed with
someone, they're not surprised or shocked. They just wait till
he gets up. What's so strange about that? So let's go . . .
(*The telephone rings*)
The hell with it. Let it ring!

MADAME ROSE

(*Moves to answer the telephone; he tries to stop her; a
brief struggle, slightly hysterical on her part. She breaks
away and gets to the phone and lifts the receiver*)
It's the Russian ambassador. He's below in the hall. Very
urgent and important.

LUMUMBA

Hell. This particular bastard is the particular bastard I *have*
to see right now.

MADAME ROSE
(*Speaking into telephone*)
Show him up. (*To* LUMUMBA)Patrice, you'd better meet him
at the top of the stairs and take him into the salon across the
landing . . .

LUMUMBA

Why?

[70]

MADAME ROSE

Oh Patrice! This room!

LUMUMBA

What about it? . . . I suppose the Congolese are the last
people a Congolese Prime Minister has to think about. It's to
the foreign ambassadors he must suit his ways. So he mustn't
go to bed without their permission. (*He puts his feet on desk
and shuts his eyes in attitude of complete exhaustion*)
(*Enter* SERVANT)

SERVANT

His Excellency, the Ambassador of the Soviet Union!
(*Enter* AMBASSADOR, *a ponderous and rather dreary
figure with wide trousers. He looks round with horror at
the scene: the smashed glassware, the sword stuck in the
middle of the carpeted floor, the apparently sleeping* LU-
MUMBA, *the flushed and slightly disheveled* MADAME ROSE.
He inhales, obviously noting the smell of spilled beer)

AMBASSADOR

(*To* MADAME ROSE)

Is he . . . ? Can he be . . . ?

MADAME ROSE

The Prime Minister is extremely fatigued, your Excellency.
He has been without regular sleep for several days. The crisis
has naturally told on him. (*Touches* LUMUMBA *on the shoulder*)
Mr. Prime Minister . . . The Soviet Ambassador . . .

LUMUMBA

(*Opens his eyes. Now quite cool and collected, he greets
the* SOVIET AMBASSADOR)

[71]

Good afternoon, Excellency. Very good of you to come over.
Won't you sit down? You have some news for me?

AMBASSADOR

I have good news, Mr. Prime Minister. I have positive
response of Soviet Government to your request for technical
aid to end secession of Katanga by expelling Western imperialist mercenaries.

LUMUMBA

Positive response! Very good . . . How positive?

AMBASSADOR

There is schedule, Mr. Prime Minister, of materiel and personnel to be furnished by Soviet Union, with estimated dates
of delivery. (*Hands* LUMUMBA *a paper*)

LUMUMBA
(*Reads*)

Transport aircraft . . . Pilots for them . . . Lorries . . .
That's about it. No bombers, Ambassador? No fighters? No
tanks? No armored cars?

AMBASSADOR
(*Stiffly*)

Mr. Prime Minister, Soviet Government does not send what
you think you want, it sends what it decides you need. Its
deliberations are systematic, its assessments are scientific, its
decisions are conclusive. This paper therefore represents what
you actually need in full, so that everything you need is being
supplied by the Soviet Government. Nothing will be subtracted,
nothing requires to be added.

LUMUMBA

I see. Do I take it that this materiel will be entirely at my disposal . . . for the transport of troops into Kasai and Katanga?

AMBASSADOR

Yes, Mr. Prime Minister.

LUMUMBA

Well, it's something. I thank your Government, Ambassador, for sending me what it decides I need. I can only hope the Soviet Government is right about what I need. I take it there is no point in my pressing for more?

AMBASSADOR

No, Mr. Prime Minister, to press for more would only be again to declare what you think you want. But this is not point since what you actually need has already been determined by Soviet Government. Deliberations of Soviet Government are systematic . . .

LUMUMBA

Thank you, Excellency, you already explained about that. Well, there doesn't seem much more to be said, does there?

AMBASSADOR

Do I understand, Mr. Prime Minister, that you wish me to carry to Chairman of Committee of Ministers of Soviet Union, Nikita S. Khrushchev, your personal greetings, and grateful acknowledgment for his fraternal aid?

LUMUMBA

Yes, Excellency. Do give him fraternal greetings . . . Fraternal, that's it. Wait a moment. I have something for him. (*He rummages in drawer and produces photograph which he proceeds to inscribe*) "To my brother Nikita with love — Patrice." There you are.

(*Hands him the photograph*)

AMBASSADOR
(*Looking at photograph, stiffly*)
Thank you. Goodbye, Mr. Prime Minister.
(*Bows to* MADAME ROSE *without speaking. Exits, holding photograph at arm's length*)

LUMUMBA
Do Russians have special legs?

MADAME ROSE
Special legs?

LUMUMBA
Yes, you know — huge and puffy . . . or else all covered with knobs — or constructed in some kind of zigzag . . . If they haven't got special legs, why would they wear trousers like that? After all, we know they never do anything without (*Mimicking*) "systematic deliberations."
(*They both laugh*)

MADAME ROSE
(*Seriously*)
All the same, Patrice, things could hardly be worse. The Russians are giving you just enough help to provoke the Americans against you; and they're not giving you enough to beat your enemies in the Congo . . . Patrice, I'm more frightened than ever!

LUMUMBA

It's disappointing. But it's better than nothing. And what else can I do? Who else can I turn to?

MADAME ROSE

Patrice, you are a Congolese revolutionary. It was the voice of the Congolese revolution that spoke through you on June thirtieth and raised the storm that is now raging all round us.

LUMUMBA

Yes, and why wouldn't a revolutionary look for help from the Russian Communists?

MADAME ROSE

Because the Russian Communists are not revolutionaries. The fact that people once had a revolution doesn't mean they are revolutionaries. If it did, the Americans, the English and the French would all be revolutionaries. These Russians will give you some encouragement, but when things get rough they will drop you. If they provoke the Americans to . . . to work against you, they will be quite happy. They want to be the friend of the African, but on the cheap. They want to cash in on your name, and on the love of the people for you. And, oh, Patrice, I am so so afraid! I am afraid it is not only your name they need, but *the memory of your name,* a name that will have become the name of a martyr . . .

LUMUMBA

Even if it were so — and it may be — what can I do? Perhaps after all, they are right. I may be more use as a martyr than as a prime minister. (*Chuckles*) There's one thing sure: I'll be a damn sight better behaved. I bet I make a nice, tidy

[75]

martyr: no drink, no hemp, no women. Example to the young.

MADAME ROSE

Patrice, please don't joke about that. Save yourself.

LUMUMBA

All right. Don't mind if I do. But how, dear Rose, but how?

MADAME ROSE

Don't rely on outside help, which only attracts more hatred
and danger. You are a Congolese; your closeness to the Congolese is your strength. Rely on the Congolese.

LUMUMBA

Well, I love them — or I love a lot of them — but *rely* on
them? I am a Congolese revolutionary, as you say, but where's
the Congolese revolution? Round the corner maybe, but it's
not a corner I'm ever going to get round. It's true, Rose, my
closeness to the people is my strength; my only strength. But
to keep it I have to talk in the language it wants to hear from
its leaders: the language of bold defiant gestures with a look of
strength about them. For these gestures a price has to be
paid: that's why people regard them as bold. Bringing in the
United Nations was such a gesture; it caught people's imagination: it made them think I had force to back me up. Then
Tshombe's backers showed them I hadn't; after Hammarskjöld's visit to Elisabethville, I had to react speedily and
dramatically or be ruined in the eyes of my people. And what
other dramatic action was open to me except the appeal to
these people? It may be a losing card, but it was the only one in
my hand that could just possibly win. And I've played it, Rose.
I've played it, and they know I've played it. You're a gambler's

moll, Rose, whether you like it or not, and it's no use telling
your gambler he oughtn't to play cards or that he ought to get
better ones. He had to take the cards he was dealt, and he
gambled on them to the limit. Is his moll still with him, while
the going is good?

MADAME ROSE
(*Softly*)

Yes, Patrice, whatever the going, whatever the gambler's
cards, whatever the cards in the other men's hands — the cards
we don't yet see. And the moll won't squeal, and she won't nag
any more . . . Patrice, what's this it was that you were suggesting when we were interrupted by that man with the funny
trousers?

LUMUMBA
(*Laughing*)

Let's go!

(*They dance out of the room*)

Scene Two

Leopoldville. Garden of the American Embassy. Later the same evening. American Ambassador, Hammarskjöld.

AMBASSADOR

"Whom the gods wish to destroy . . ."

HAMMARSKJÖLD

The gods?

AMBASSADOR

Or their instruments.

(*Enter* THIRD SECRETARY)

THIRD SECRETARY

(*To* AMBASSADOR)

The cable is decoded, sir. I have it here. It's on the subject matter of your discussion with the Secretary-General. Will you read it now, sir?

AMBASSADOR

Yes.

(*Takes the decoded cable and begins to read it*)

THIRD SECRETARY

(*To Hammarskjöld*)

The first Russian transports are due in in thirty-six hours.

What are the U.N. forces at Leopoldville Airport going to do, sir?

HAMMARSKJÖLD

Do?

THIRD SECRETARY

About the Russians.

HAMMARSKJÖLD

The U.N. forces have no mandate to do anything about them. The U.N. forces are here only to help the Congolese Government in certain specific ways. The Russians, like the U.N. forces themselves, will be here by invitation of the Congolese Government.

THIRD SECRETARY

Isn't that rather — legalistic, sir, in this crisis?

HAMMARSKJÖLD

If "legalistic" means respectful of the Charter and the decisions of the Security Council, then I am happy to be legalistic.

AMBASSADOR

(*Looking up from cable*)

You may leave us, Armitage. Oh, and Armitage . . . If you again feel the urge to play high diplomacy, go and play it with one of the other Third Secretaries, will you? And leave my guests alone.

THIRD SECRETARY

(*Miserably*)

Yes, sir.

[79]

(*Exit* THIRD SECRETARY)

AMBASSADOR
(*To* HAMMARSKJÖLD)
That is a very tedious young man. He has, however, one useful quality. He reflects with uncanny accuracy the feelings and ideas of the kind of people who give me my instructions . . . Your reply to him, Dag, was a model of textbook orthodoxy, as he deserved. I take it, however, that it's not the answer you would feel bound to give *me* in reply to — somewhat similar questions?

HAMMARSKJÖLD
Of course not, Kevin. You and I obviously have to talk about the situation.

AMBASSADOR
We do, Dag, we do . . . As you will have guessed, this telegram is a pressing one. It requires action. As far as Russians in the Congo are concerned, Washington makes it clear that they will not permit that. Whatever is necessary to stop it — they say — must be done. Whatever is necessary . . . Three rather disquieting little words, don't you think?

HAMMARSKJÖLD
I do indeed . . . Why should they feel quite so strongly as that about the Congo?

AMBASSADOR
One would need to ask Armitage . . . Oh, if we bothered to ask we would get answers. Voluminous ones. Strategic imperatives first of all. The Pentagon has wads of paper to prove

the unique, superlative, transcendental strategic importance of
any patch of territory that may at any time turn up in the news.
And to be fair, this is a very big patch of territory, with important resources in strategic minerals and two major air bases.
But that's not really the point. The point is that the political
party now in power in my country helped itself to get there by
yelling that the other party "lost China." That being so, they
cannot afford to allow the other party a chance to yell that *they*
have lost the Congo. Of course, you and I, who know the
Congo, know that to lose the Congo is something earnestly to
be desired. But the American electorate, who know nothing
about the Congo except that it is big and in the news, would
feel frightened if they were suddenly told that they had lost
the Congo. And because they feel that way, and because of
how the Administration feels about how the electorate feel we
have reached the stage of "whatever is necessary." That is to
say, the stage of fast tough action.

HAMMARSKJÖLD

We have reached that stage, Kevin?

AMBASSADOR

I was speaking of us Americans. On our own, if necessary.
But I think I can show you some reasons why you might feel it
to be in the long term interests of the U.N., and of peace, to
work with us . . .

HAMMARSKJÖLD

Go on.

AMBASSADOR

First of all, we, the United States, have decided, for our own inscrutable reasons, that we must throw the Russians out of the Congo. Right? No point now in arguing is it wise, is it right and all that. We're grown men. The decision is now a fact of international life — a big explosive fact, ticking away between us here . . . Now the awkward thing, of course, is that the Russians, whom we have to throw out, have been invited in by the perfectly legitimate head of a government which we recognize. So what is, as my telegram says, "necessary"?

HAMMARSKJÖLD

You must engineer the fall of Prime Minister Lumumba. And you must ensure that his successor will invite the Russians out and also that, if necessary, he will invite you in.

AMBASSADOR

Right. And by the way, we are prepared to come in if necessary. Horse, foot and artillery. If they really want another Korea they can have another Korea. This time on much more favorable terms from our point of view. Our military chiefs are quite enthusiastic about the logistics of this particular local war.

HAMMARSKJÖLD

I'm sure they are . . . And are the arrangements for the fall of Lumumba already complete?

AMBASSADOR

Up to a point. That's to say that President Kasavubu, whom our Treasury has supplied with arguments that he found convincing, is agreeable to saying, at a moment to be agreed on, that he dismisses Lumumba, and that he appoints in his place Joseph Iléo, who is our man and will do what we say. Whether

Kasavubu has a constitutional right to do all or any of this is debatable. And will be debated. But the important thing from our point of view is that our lawyers and our public relations people — working together of course — will be able to prove that the transaction was constitutionally impeccable —

HAMMARSKJÖLD

To *prove* that?

AMBASSADOR

To the satisfaction of our own people. So that legitimacy is secured — which is very important for us. So that whatever we have to do in the Congo henceforward will be legitimate because it will be done at the request of the legitimate Prime Minister of the Congo, Joseph Iléo . . .

HAMMARSKJÖLD

Tell me, Kevin, does your Government expect the U.N. to dress up your Korea in the Congo? To supply blue hats and a blue flag to cover a U.S. action with U.N. stage props? If so, it's not to be had. The Soviets won't miss their chance of a veto in the Security Council this time. And you no longer have the votes in the General Assembly. *And* you don't have a Secretary-General who will play ball on this. I'm not Trygve Lie.

AMBASSADOR

Come on, Dag, we're not that dumb. We're not inviting *you* to that kind of a ball game. Whatever our military chiefs may hope, we're not trying to make a Korea in the Congo. We're trying to avoid one. And it's for that, and only that that we want your help.

[83]

HAMMARSKJÖLD

Well?

AMBASSADOR

With your help it can be a short, clean, almost bloodless crisis. If you support us, the Soviets will back away, before they get deeply involved. But if you hesitate, or go in for ostentatious neutrality, they may be drawn in deep, and if *they* are, *we* most certainly will, and there's your Korea. I agree that it will be a Korea without the U.N. Very well. But what does that mean? It will mean *either* that our people will fight the war in the presence of a passive noncombatant U.N. force, *or* that the U.N. force will pack its bags and go home. And either way, what do you think will be left of the United Nations? It will be regarded universally as having ignominiously failed. It will altogether lose all public support in the United States, and you know what that would mean. It will be hopelessly discredited, crippled and impotent — in a worse state than the League was after Abyssinia. And then what? With a Korea in the heart of Africa, with the United Nations incapacitated, and the paths of mediation blocked, the chances will be higher than they have ever been that we shall drift to world war. Well, Dag, what do you choose?

HAMMARSKJÖLD

The context you make for me is such that if I am to save the United Nations, and the peace, I must help you to destroy Patrice Lumumba.

AMBASSADOR

Dead right, Dag, dead right. And let us proceed with our eyes wide open. When we say "destroy," that is what we mean literally. Oh, we're not going to murder him ourselves; we don't have to. But he will remain a danger for us as long as he lives, because he is a fantastically attractive man, and dynamic and intelligent in his own weird way. And the political Congo that we shall bring to existence after the crash of *his* Congo will be one where all power is in the hands of his enemies, chosen because they are his enemies. We cannot allow him to leave the Congo, and stir up trouble for us elsewhere in Africa. And we are not going to protect him effectively inside the Congo. And you are not going to protect him either, or not for long. You cannot provide him with a bodyguard while he goes round preaching revolution, and risking again the whole Korean sequence. No, you and I — if you agree — having thrown Patrice Lumumba to his enemies, will then stand aside while those enemies, chosen by us, put him to death. We shall be accused of having his blood on our hands, and we shall vehemently and plausibly deny that, and his blood will remain on our hands. If it's clean hands you want, Dag, have nothing to do with my proposition . . . Well, what do you say? Do you accept? Do you vote for the death of Patrice Lumumba?

HAMMARSKJÖLD

I do. The logic of the situation you have constructed leaves me no choice. If, in order to save the United Nations and perhaps world peace, I must acquiesce in the death of one rash man, who summoned up forces that he did not understand, then I must acquiesce in the death of that man. I do not think that I can pass through that unscathed — spiritually or even perhaps physically. But it is not my business to remain unscathed, or to keep my hands clean. It is my business to defend the hopes that humanity has placed in the United Nations. (*After a break*) And I did try to save him . . .

AMBASSADOR

You did, Dag, and this is where you stop trying. The decision in principle is taken. Now for the tactics. The key to the situation is the radio . . .

Scene Three

Leopoldville, 10–14 September 1960. A bare, dark stage with two spotlit microphones. A broad blue line left center indicates the River Congo. All the action takes place to the right of this line, except when indicated. One microphone is to the left of the line. The characters stand still on stage and speak as they are spotlit. First Representative of the Secretary-General, Second Representative of the Secretary-General, Joseph Kasavubu, Joseph Mobutu, Lumumba, U.N. soldiers; later a Singer, women, Congolese soldiers, First White Man, Second White Man. The two Representatives hold the front of the stage on either side, framing the rest of the action. They speak impassively.

FIRST REPRESENTATIVE

We are the Representatives of the Secretary-General. We represent, that is to say, his interpretation of the resolutions of the Security Council.

SECOND REPRESENTATIVE

We represent a certain international consensus. We are that consensus made flesh. (*To the audience*) You must think of us as *your* representatives. We hope we shall give satisfaction.

FIRST REPRESENTATIVE

That is the philosophy of it. Technically, our mission is to extend military assistance to the Government of the Congo at

[87]

its invitation. For the moment, in the rather strange circumstances which we think you know about, this assistance must take the form of bringing down the Government in question.

(*The Representatives each take* KASAVUBU *by an arm and lead him to the microphone right*)

KASAVUBU

(*At microphone, reads in entirely wooden tone, occasionally stumbling over his text*)

I, Joseph Kasavubu, President of the Congo, in virtue of the powers wasted — vested in me by the Constitution of the Congo, hereby make a very important announcement. The Lord Mayor, Patrice Lumumba, who was appointed by the King of the Belgians in accordance with the provisions of the Fund — Fundamental Law — has betrayed the task entrusted to him. He has had recourse to arbitrary measures which have produced discord among the Government and the people. He has deprived numerous citizens of Fun — of Fundamental Liberties. And now he is hurling the country into an atrocious civil war. For these reasons I have judged it necessary to dismiss the Government immediately, in virtue of the constitutional powers conferred on me, and I nominate Mr. Joseph Iléo as Prime Minister. Mr. Iléo has the responsibility to form a new Government. I swear to see to it that all the inhabitants of our country shall be ded — shall be dedicated henceforward to the progress of the country in peace and concord . . . I ask the United Nations to assume responsibility for maintaining order and peace.

FIRST REPRESENTATIVE

The United Nations will accept this responsibility.

SECOND REPRESENTATIVE

But in the meantime we must listen to Mr. Lumumba . . .

FIRST REPRESENTATIVE

Just once more . . .

LUMUMBA

(*At microphone, speaking with passion and gesticulating*)

The Government rejoices in the victory which it has achieved today. Yes! A victory! Because the people of the Congo can now see who is working for it and who is working for the imperialists! who is for and who against our country! who is honest and who is not! Kasavubu, whom we believed to be a brother, has betrayed us. He has not the power to remove the Government. In a democratic country, only the Parliament has that power. We are going to convene the Parliament. In the meantime I remain Prime Minister of the Congo. I ask the United Nations not to exceed their responsibilities and not to interfere in the difficulties which have arisen between the Government and Mr. Kasavubu.

FIRST REPRESENTATIVE

The United Nations cannot exceed its responsibilities.

SECOND REPRESENTATIVE

Nor can it interfere in the internal affairs of any member nation.

(*Throughout the subsequent proceedings spotlights remain on the Representatives who stand facing the audience unless otherwise indicated. A Congolese woman* SINGER, *strikingly beautiful and strongly built, takes her place at the microphone, right; with her, a band. Perform-*

ance of the cha-cha-cha "Vive Lumumba Patrice, Vive Patrice Lumumba")

SINGER

Now we are going to hear the voice of our great, our beloved Prime Minister himself, our dear Patrice Lumumba!

(*Members of the band applaud and start "Vive Patrice Lumumba." A little more of the cha-cha-cha.* SINGER *continues*)

We are going to hear a recording of the great, beautiful speech in which Patrice unmasked the traitors who want to sell our country back to the imperialists.

(*Band applauds; more cha-cha-cha*)

FIRST REPRESENTATIVE

No, they are not going to hear that great beautiful speech.

(*He turns to face the group and the microphone, right. U.N. soldiers begin to converge on that group. The cha-cha-cha continues. The* SECOND REPRESENTATIVE *turns to face the group at the microphone. He slowly raises his right hand. The soldiers raise their weapons. The band stops playing. There is a moment of silence*)

SINGER

(*At microphone, starts again to sing, slowly and defiantly*)

Vive Patrice Lumumba! Vive . . .

(*A soldier seizes her and bundles her, struggling and screaming, into the darkness, where her screams die away. The soldiers move towards the band, who scramble off into safety. The soldiers group themselves around the microphone.* THE REPRESENTATIVES *turn to face the audience again*)

FIRST REPRESENTATIVE

Some of you may be wondering how the little scene you have just witnessed may be reconciled with our undertaking not to interfere in the internal affairs of the Congo. The answer is as follows: The United Nations undertook at the very outset to provide the Government of the Congo with such military assistance as may be necessary — Security Council Resolution S/4387 of July 14, 1960. President Kasavubu, as you heard just now, defined the form of military assistance which is required, by asking the U.N. to assume responsibility for maintaining order and peace. The U.N. has agreed to assume this responsibility.

SECOND REPRESENTATIVE

That is a perfectly valid answer, on the plane of legality. In a wider perspective there are compelling reasons, both ethical and political, for the action we have been obliged to take. The type of broadcast which you have just heard Mr. Lumumba make, involving emotional appeals of various kinds and violent accusations of treachery directed against the Head of State, constitutes a threat to order and peace.

FIRST REPRESENTATIVE

Its action does not in any sense constitute an interference in the internal affairs of the Congo, nor has the United Nations departed from its policy of strict neutrality as regards the dispute between President Kasavubu —

[91]

SECOND REPRESENTATIVE

Whose authority as Head of State none of you, I imagine, will be disposed to challenge —

FIRST REPRESENTATIVE

— and Mr. Patrice Lumumba.

(LUMUMBA *approaches the microphone, right, and is stopped by the* SERGEANT)

SERGEANT

I'm sorry, sir, the station is closed. No admission for anyone except U.N. personnel.

LUMUMBA

I am the Prime Minister, the Head of the Government of the Congo. This is the Radio of the Government of the Congo. Get out of my way. (*He tries to force his way past the* SERGEANT. *Two U.N. soldiers pick him up and carry him into the darkness, struggling silently*)

FIRST REPRESENTATIVE

A painful and undignified scene.

SECOND REPRESENTATIVE

And unnecessary. Because Radio Leopoldville is closed not only to Mr. Lumumba, whom you have seen making this rather flamboyant protest, but to President Kasavubu himself, who has accepted the United Nations decision with his usual dignity and composure.

FIRST REPRESENTATIVE

Nothing, indeed, brings out more clearly the absolute neutrality of the United Nations than this.

SECOND REPRESENTATIVE

The Radio is closed —

FIRST REPRESENTATIVE

Both to Mr. Lumumba —

SECOND REPRESENTATIVE

And to President Kasavubu —

FIRST REPRESENTATIVE

Impartially.

(KASAVUBU *at the microphone, left, which has hitherto been in darkness; now spotlit. He speaks with a drum accompaniment*)

KASAVUBU

I, Kasavubu, am President of the Congo! The Prime Minister of the Congo is Joseph Iléo! I, Kasavubu, am President of the Congo! The Prime Minister of the Congo is Joseph Iléo. I, Kasavubu, am President of the Congo.

(*His voice fades out but the spotlight remains on him during the next few speeches and the drumming continues at the same rhythm and his lips continue to move*)

FIRST REPRESENTATIVE

A very clear message.

SECOND REPRESENTATIVE

You might find it a little monotonous —

FIRST REPRESENTATIVE

But the President is an African.

[93]

SECOND REPRESENTATIVE

He knows his people.

FIRST REPRESENTATIVE

Perhaps you may be wondering what he is doing out there . . .

SECOND REPRESENTATIVE

And how he comes, after all, to be talking on the radio.

FIRST REPRESENTATIVE

An interesting point.

SECOND REPRESENTATIVE

Happy to clear it up. (*Turning and pointing*) That blue line you see there is the Congo river. That place over there, where the other radio is, just across the river from us here in Leopoldville is called Brazzaville.

FIRST REPRESENTATIVE

It used, until very recently, to be called the capital of the French Congo, as Leopoldville used to be the capital of the Belgian Congo.

SECOND REPRESENTATIVE

Now with this tremendously rapid progress of emancipation we have been having recently, both cities have become capitals of separate and independent States, just divided by this river.

FIRST REPRESENTATIVE

The Government over there have an admiration for President Kasavubu's qualities . . .

SECOND REPRESENTATIVE

As a statesman . . .

FIRST REPRESENTATIVE

And for this reason they have allowed him the use of their transmitter . . .

SECOND REPRESENTATIVE

. . . which happens to be an extremely powerful one . . .

FIRST REPRESENTATIVE

. . . so that President Kasavubu's voice can be heard at present all over the Congo. Lumumba's voice on the other hand cannot be heard on any radio.

(*A pause during which, to a distant drum accompaniment,* KASAVUBU's *voice can be heard faintly repeating the message of his previous speech*)

SECOND REPRESENTATIVE

Why doesn't Lumumba, too, speak from Brazzaville?

FIRST REPRESENTATIVE

Well, you see, they just don't like him over there. The Head of State in Brazzaville — the Abbé Fulbert Youlou — happens to be a close friend and ally of Mr. Moïse Tshombe, the President of Katanga.

SECOND REPRESENTATIVE

Mr. Lumumba has been in the habit of reviling both these gentlemen as traitors, lackeys, imperialist stooges, and so on, so that naturally he would not be welcome in Brazzaville, any more than in Elisabethville.

He would not be safe in Brazzaville, any more than in Elisabethville.

(*A pause — distant drumming*)

SECOND REPRESENTATIVE
So the net result is that President Kasavubu is on the air and Mr. Lumumba is not.

FIRST REPRESENTATIVE
And this has come about without any departure by the United Nations from its policy of the most strict neutrality.

SECOND REPRESENTATIVE
You surely would not expect us to interfere with the movements of President Kasavubu.

FIRST REPRESENTATIVE
You ask, what about Lumumba's movements? Well, that's another interesting question. The United Nations have been obliged to take control of the airports of the Congo. In accordance with the responsibilities which they have assumed for order and peace they must decide whether or not to authorize movements of particular individuals.

SECOND REPRESENTATIVE
Those movements which are conducive to peace and order must — in accordance with our criteria — be authorized. And these include the movements of President Kasavubu, Mr. Iléo, and people of that sort — movements which as a matter of experience we know to be tranquilizing.

FIRST REPRESENTATIVE

On the other hand we have the duty to prevent movements which are disruptive of peace and order. And again we know from experience that the movements of Mr. Lumumba and his friends fall into this category.

SECOND REPRESENTATIVE

So in practice we allow Mr. Iléo and his friends to travel, while we prevent Mr. Lumumba and his friends from doing so.

FIRST REPRESENTATIVE

I know this will seem to some of you discriminatory, a departure from our principle of strict impartiality and so on. It is particularly easy for people thousands of miles away from the scene to reason in this way. I assure you, if you were here in Leopoldville at this time you would think — and above all *feel* — very differently about it all.

SECOND REPRESENTATIVE

Because you see here, in Leopoldville, Mr. Lumumba is still at liberty, and even confirmed in office by his Parliament . . . His voice can still be heard, not on the radio, but in the streets . . .

LUMUMBA

(*Voice offstage, faint but clear*)

Men and women of the Congo! Arise in your might! Awake! You are being betrayed! Your birthright is being stolen! The white men and the black traitors want to enslave you again! Women of the Congo, arouse your menfolk, denounce the traitors! Men of the Congo, find the traitors, the friends of

[97]

Kasavubu white or black, and kill them! Soldiers of the Congo, if your officers will not do their duty, shoot them down and rally to your Government! The Lumumba Government is still the Government of the Congo!

(*Cries of "Lumumba! Lumumba! Down with Kasavubu! Death to the traitors! Down with the U.N.!" A group of women dressed in white crosses the stage from the left, led by the* SINGER. *They carry green branches and wave them rhythmically while they sing the Lumumba song. As they move upstage right, a single shot is heard. Two white men enter running — white shirts, shorts. The women turn to face the white men, forming a solid line before which the men hesitate. A second shot is heard. The* FIRST WHITE MAN *— young and well-built — jumps forward and manages to force his way past the women. He leaves his shirt behind and a woman starts to dance with this. The women laugh. A third shot is heard*)

SECOND WHITE MAN
(*Small, puny, elderly*)

Please, ladies! Please let me pass. I am only a small man — no politics! I have three grandchildren! Please!

(*A fourth shot. Male voices shouting "Traitors! Kill!" Two of the women move apart, to let the old man through. As the old man darts forward, the* SINGER *catches him by the arm and hurls him back. Enter three Congolese soldiers. The* FIRST SOLDIER *carries a revolver, the* SECOND SOLDIER *a rifle. Both of these are in conventional military attire. The* THIRD SOLDIER *is naked to the waist and obviously drunk. He holds his belt in one hand, a bottle of beer in the other. The old man turns to face the soldiers*)

[98]

FIRST SOLDIER

Your papers!

(*The old man fumbles in his pocket*)

THIRD SOLDIER

Do you like beer?

SECOND WHITE MAN

(*Timidly*)

Yes. I do.

(*The* THIRD SOLDIER *hits the old man on the head with the bottle. As the old man falls to the ground, the* THIRD SOLDIER *starts beating him with his belt. The* FIRST SOLDIER *shoots the old man as he lies on the ground. The* SECOND SOLDIER *fires three shots in the direction of the audience, and all three men run back in the direction from which they came. The women are silent for a moment looking down at the body. Then the* SINGER *starts again to sing the Lumumba song very loudly and defiantly. The other women take up the song more quietly and file out, the* SINGER *remaining to the last. Just before she leaves, she gently drops her green branch on the body of the old man*)

FIRST REPRESENTATIVE

You will realize that nobody responsible for peace and order could permit such conditions to continue. Our responsibilities in this domain therefore oblige us to cooperate very closely with those who are committed to the restoration of order.

SECOND REPRESENTATIVE

In practice this also means those who are committed to the

suppression or at least the silencing of Mr. Patrice Lumumba, whose continued political activity is incompatible with peace and order. President Kasavubu, unfortunately, has not proved strong enough to restore order and we have been obliged to look elsewhere.

FIRST REPRESENTATIVE

You will observe the way in which we are drawn, by our proper responsibilities and by these alone, into actions which look like, but are really not, acts of interference in the internal affairs of the Congo.

SECOND REPRESENTATIVE

To be a little more specific, we have just paid five million francs from U.N. funds to Colonel Joseph Mobutu. And Colonel Mobutu is about to make an important announcement . . .

(*Spotlight on* COLONEL MOBUTU, *who moves to the microphone, right. The U.N. guard salutes him smartly as he passes them to take his stand at the microphone*)

MOBUTU

(*At microphone*)

The Congolese National Army has decided to neutralize the Head of State, the Lumumba Government, the Iléo Government and the two Houses of Parliament. This is not a military coup d'état. Long live the Congo! Long live the Congolese National Army!

(*When the characters leave, the* REPRESENTATIVES *take the center of the stage*)

FIRST REPRESENTATIVE

Colonel Mobutu also now expels the Soviet Embassy, and

[100]

the Czechoslovak Embassy. Colonel Mobutu's Government
thereby assures itself of the goodwill and support of the Western governments and especially of the United States.

SECOND REPRESENTATIVE

As for Lumumba he will be driven to seek the protection of
the United Nations, and this will be accorded to him —

FIRST REPRESENTATIVE

A little too zealously perhaps.

SECOND REPRESENTATIVE

By a gentleman who is about to take over from us here —

FIRST REPRESENTATIVE

An Indian gentleman.

SECOND REPRESENTATIVE

Because we are about to leave the stage, you see.

FIRST REPRESENTATIVE

The Congo stage.

SECOND REPRESENTATIVE

And the United Nations Stage.

FIRST REPRESENTATIVE

In brief, the stage.

SECOND REPRESENTATIVE

You see, our usefulness . . .

[101]

FIRST REPRESENTATIVE

Is exhausted.

(*Both* REPRESENTATIVES *bow their heads*)

SECOND REPRESENTATIVE

It is exhausted;

FIRST REPRESENTATIVE

But it was useful.

SECOND REPRESENTATIVE

Our actions were entirely within the United Nations mandate.

FIRST REPRESENTATIVE

But they were also necessarily somewhat drastic, and open to misrepresentation.

SECOND REPRESENTATIVE

They have aroused resentment among certain member nations . . .

FIRST REPRESENTATIVE

Especially in Africa and Asia.

SECOND REPRESENTATIVE

As the support of these nations is essential to our Chief, the Secretary-General, in carrying out his tasks especially in the Congo, we have become an embarrassment.

FIRST REPRESENTATIVE

We shall be dropped.

SECOND REPRESENTATIVE
Mr. Hammarskjöld will defend us publicly

FIRST REPRESENTATIVE
But he will disavow us privately

SECOND REPRESENTATIVE
In appropriate company

FIRST REPRESENTATIVE
Among Africans and Asians

SECOND REPRESENTATIVE
And he will replace us forthwith

FIRST REPRESENTATIVE
By an Indian gentleman.

SECOND REPRESENTATIVE
It will be understood that it is because we exceeded our instructions

FIRST REPRESENTATIVE
That we exhausted our usefulness

SECOND REPRESENTATIVE
But in fact it was not excess that led to our exhaustion

FIRST REPRESENTATIVE
Not excess, but success. We did what was required of us.

SECOND REPRESENTATIVE

It is true that the Secretary-General whom we have faithfully represented . . .

FIRST REPRESENTATIVE

. . . Neither knew nor wished to know the details of our transactions.

SECOND REPRESENTATIVE

But everything we did was in full accord with his directives on policy . . .

FIRST REPRESENTATIVE

. . . Which as it happens were themselves in full accord . . .

SECOND REPRESENTATIVE

. . . With the policy of our own country.
(*A pause*)

FIRST REPRESENTATIVE

We should perhaps have mentioned before

SECOND REPRESENTATIVE

That as well as being impartial officials of the United Nations . . .
(*Produces United Nations flag*)

FIRST REPRESENTATIVE

We are also loyal citizens of the United States.
(*Produces United States flag*)

SECOND REPRESENTATIVE

Loyal? Impartial? American? International?

FIRST REPRESENTATIVE

To serve the United Nations, or to serve one nation?

BOTH REPRESENTATIVES

(*In unison, solemnly and with emphasis*)

We have the solution:

THE SERVICE OF ONE IS THE SERVICE OF ALL

(*Repeat*)

THE SERVICE OF ONE IS THE SERVICE OF ALL

FIRST REPRESENTATIVE

Always provided, of course, that you serve *the right one.*

SECOND REPRESENTATIVE

But we know the right one

FIRST REPRESENTATIVE

And we serve it in the interests of all.

SECOND REPRESENTATIVE

The apparent incompatibility between the service of the United Nations, and the service of *a* nation is thus automatically transcended, as far as people in our position are concerned.

FIRST REPRESENTATIVE

In serving the United Nations, we have simultaneously attained a major policy objective of our own country: the elimination of Communist influence from the Congo.

SECOND REPRESENTATIVE

We go into retirement, therefore, without repining.

[105]

FIRST REPRESENTATIVE

Having found in the course of our duties

SECOND REPRESENTATIVE

Fulfillment and harmony

FIRST REPRESENTATIVE

To a degree perhaps somewhat unusual in the lives of . . .

BOTH REPRESENTATIVES
(*With gravity*)

International Civil Servants
(*They exchange and re-exchange their flags*)

ACT THREE

ACT THREE

Scene One

Two and a half months later. A room in a villa at Leopold-
ville. On a sofa Pauline Lumumba is weeping and Madame
Rose is comforting her. Patrice Lumumba and Asdal are talk-
ing at a table. Lumumba seems older and grimmer.

LUMUMBA

(*Earnestly*)

All I'm asking you for, Rajat, is to authorize this yourself — on compassionate grounds — without referring it to
Hammarskjöld.

ASDAL

(*Gently*)

I'm sorry, Patrice, I'm willing to *recommend* it on compassionate grounds, but not to authorize it myself. It's too big.
I'm not here to take major decisions in my own right. I'm a
representative of the Secretary-General, lent to him by the
Government of India — to which also I have certain responsibilities in the longer term.

LUMUMBA

(*Bitterly*)

You represent this and have responsibilities to that. I am
a father whose daughter is dead and you refuse me permission
to attend her burial . . .

(PAULINE LUMUMBA *shrieks and rocks on* MADAME ROSE'S *arms*)

ASDAL
(Still gently)
I don't refuse you permission. Technically, you are free to
go at your own risk. But I cannot provide you with a U.N. aircraft. If you attempt to go by road you will almost certainly be
arrested and then face trial and execution, perhaps execution
without trial, by Mobutu's Government.

LUMUMBA
Very well, I shall go by road.

MADAME ROSE
No Patrice, for God's sake, no!
(PAULINE *looks around, apparently dazed*)

MADAME ROSE
(*To* ASDAL)
You must stop him. You cannot allow him to commit sui-
cide . . .

LUMUMBA
(*Gently and sadly, turning to face her, and taking her
hand in his*)
It's no use, Rose. Pauline understands this better. Her grief
for our daughter's death and for my death are one grief. She
knows what I must do because she feels the same as I feel, as
you cannot do. She knows there is nothing she can do about
either death except cry her heart out . . .
(*Kisses her hand, relinquishes it and turns back to*
ASDAL. ROSE *turns away, stricken*)

[110]

ASDAL

All the same, Madame Rose is right, suicide is what it would
be.

PAULINE

Rose, dear!

MADAME ROSE
(*Going to her; quietly*)
Yes, Pauline?

PAULINE

Rose, I think I could drink some hot coffee now. Could you
get me some?

MADAME ROSE

I'll get it right away.
(PAULINE *wraps her cloth around her head, curls up on
the sofa and goes to sleep. Exit* MADAME ROSE)

LUMUMBA

All right, if you want to avoid the suicide, let me have a
seat on an aircraft to Stanleyville. Or take me to Stanleyville
under guard. Either way I'd be very happy. I don't absolutely
insist on having my throat cut, you know.

ASDAL

That I would have to put to Hammarskjöld. And I am afraid
he would think this was just an excuse for getting to Stanleyville to lead the rebels — well, to lead your friends there.

LUMUMBA
(*Bitterly*)
Yes, of course, dead daughters have no significance in inter-

[111]

national politics. Therefore dead daughters do not exist. Therefore they can only be a fiction to cover something political, which alone is real.

ASDAL

That's all very well, Patrice, but can you undertake, if you go to Stanleyville, to refrain from all political activity while there?

LUMUMBA

(*Roars with laughter*)

Really, the United Nations in the Congo gets funnier and funnier! "Lumumba in Stanleyville refraining from political activity. Tableau!" (*Assumes mincing air as of plaster saint*) Listen, Rajat, Lumumba in Stanleyville *cannot* refrain from what you said. Even if he wanted to — and he isn't particularly good at refraining — LUMUMBA IN STANLEYVILLE *is* political activity: powerful medicine that changes all the politics of the Congo overnight . . .

ASDAL

I know that, Patrice. And the Secretary-General knows it too. And that is why you will not get a seat in one of our aircraft, or an escort to Stanleyville. Listen, Patrice, you know where I stand on all this?

LUMUMBA

Yes, Rajat you are my friend, as far as a man in your position can be my friend. And a little further, because you have risked your position for me. And risked your life in protecting me. And U.N. soldiers, from your country and from other countries, have lost their lives because of that protection. I trust you, Rajat. Say what you have to say.

(MADAME ROSE *returns with coffee. Finding* PAULINE *asleep, she puts down the tray on a table near her, then sits down beside* LUMUMBA *at the table, listening intently to the conversation. The men pay no attention to her*)

ASDAL

The whole international position, Patrice, is about to change because of the Presidential election in the United States. And the change is wholly favorable from your point of view. The President whose decision forced Hammarskjöld to use my predecessors to bring your Government down — that President is going out and his party is losing. The new President, John Kennedy, will not be committed to the old policies, and we know that he will be attentive to African and Asian criticisms of those policies, and to African and Asian suggestions as to what should be done. That given, the whole balance of forces inside the United Nations shifts, and the Secretary-General can pursue radically new policies. These would include — I have good reason to believe — the reconvening of the Parliament of the Congo under U.N. protection. And that, as you know, would mean your reconfirmation as Prime Minister of the Congo. Kasavubu would recognize this because he does what the Americans tell him. And the United Nations will recognize it also . . .

LUMUMBA

For the same reason . . . And when will all these good things happen?

ASDAL

The new President takes office in January. The effect of

[113]

policy changes would not be felt in the Congo before March.
You could be Prime Minister again by May . . .

LUMUMBA

And in the meantime I cannot attend my daughter's burial?

ASDAL

You cannot safely attend it.

LUMUMBA

Then I will attend it unsafely.

MADAME ROSE

Patrice, please! Even if you won't protect your own life,
isn't it your duty to the Congolese people, to the Congolese
revolution, to reserve yourself for the time when you can lead
them again?

LUMUMBA

(*Smiles at her*)

Come off it, my little Rose. You don't love the Congolese
people. How could any white person love them? They don't
love white people because they have been given reason to hate
them. And the Congolese revolution? Do you really find that
so lovable? Congolese revolutionaries are simply Congolese
who have found the courage to hurt and kill white people.
Sometimes they find that courage in what they know of Communism; sometimes in schnapps or hemp. If those revolutionaries caught you, and didn't know you were my girl, they
would certainly rape you, probably kill you, and perhaps eat
you. These are ignorant and violent men and the face they

turn to you — the face you have made them turn to you — is not attractive. Yet it is not their only face. In any case, they are my people, they are my brothers, and I must be with them. If I can. Rose, do you remember telling me once I must rely on the Congolese?

MADAME ROSE
(*Sobbing*)

Yes, Patrice.

LUMUMBA

You said that for the same reason as what you said just now — that is you wanted to help me save my skin, while thinking heroic thoughts about the Congo. I thought at the time it was extraordinarily bad advice. Yet I am going to take it now. I am going out among the Congolese, among my brothers, to bury my daughter, without waiting for the permission of the Americans, or the protection of their servants of the United Nations.

ASDAL

Is it for pride that you are destroying yourself?

LUMUMBA

I am not destroying myself, I am keeping myself intact. It would be if I said to you: "No, sir, I will not bury my daughter, I will await a favorable political conjuncture!" that I would be destroying myself! I know what Hammarskjöld wants. He wants to keep me on ice. He likes ice; I don't, and I won't be kept on it. Because when he took me out of the deep freeze I would have to be a different Lumumba — Prime Minister Lumumba by the grace of President Kennedy and Secretary-General Hammarskjöld. A tidied-up, disinfected, respectable Lumumba. Right, Rajat?

ASDAL

(*Uncomfortably*)

More or less.

LUMUMBA

And the next step would be the execution of my friends, for their criminal and barbarous acts — which are not few — as an earnest of my good faith. No thanks . . . Mind you, I might well have accepted. Had my daughter not died. What is natural to me is to go to her burial, to mourn her with my brothers, and then to lead my brothers in their struggle. For you, or rather for that iceman, these are separate issues, sealed off by logical distinctions. And when the logic has worked, you find yourself saying: "No, I must not bury my daughter because then I would only lead my brothers." And so, from abandoning your dead daughter, you are led to betray your brothers and your own self. If my daughter had not called me, I would have forgotten . . . Now I am going to Stanleyville. Or towards Stanleyville. No Rose, I'm sorry, I can't bring you. (*Laughs tenderly*) The immaturity of your plumage would betray me. Goodbye, Rose. (*Kisses her, then bends over the sleeping* PAULINE *and kisses her also, then turns back to* ROSE) Listen, Rose, if things go badly — and they may not — I am not likely to be buried. (*She looks at him in horror as he goes on*) And that will hurt *her* most of all. So please make up some story for her that will make it easier — something I'm supposed to have said; anything. That you do understand — not like the Congolese revolution, God help us all! (*Kisses her again*) Goodbye, my dear.

[116]

Thanks, Rajat, and sorry about this. (*Shakes hands*) The iceman will be very upset. (*Straightens up*) Come, let me see you out. I'll call you from Stanleyville.

(*Exits with* ASDAL)

(MADAME ROSE *falls on her knees beside the sleeping* PAULINE)

Scene Two

Leopoldville. December 1960–January 1961. Stage as for Act II, Scene III, but with the microphones on each side of a cinema screen at center. Asdal, on right, at table with telephone. Mobutu and Kasavubu on either side of the news screen.

ASDAL

(At telephone)

S.G.? Yes . . . He has been captured . . . at a place called Mweka, in Kasai, on his way to Stanleyville . . . Okito, Mpolo and others were with him . . . Spotted by aircraft from across the river. Pilot? French or Belgian, I suppose — not Congolese anyway, there aren't any — S.G.? S.G.? — that you, Ralph? Please get the S.G. to the phone again — I didn't ring him just to give him the news. There's a most urgent problem about . . . Yes, his personal decision. Yes. Good. Sir? It's this: there are U.N. forces near Mweka. They are there in sufficient strength to free Lumumba . . . Yes, the line is bad, I'll repeat. *(Shouts) The U.N. forces are in sufficient strength to free Lumumba.* What's that? Again . . . No action? . . . I'm afraid we need a specific decision. You see, the U.N. commanding officer on the spot has actually *sought* authority to free Lumumba . . . Yes, *he* sought it from *us* . . . What? What nationality? These are the U.N. Ghana contingent in Kasai — you remember we sent them there to get them out of Leopoldville after . . . Yes. Sorry? What is he? What rank? Oh, I see. He's a Ghanaian —

[118]

an African, sir . . . Do we agree? Yes, sir, I support their request and wish to authorize them to free Lumumba . . . Yes, sir, I do know your official directive and can repeat it: it is "to refrain from any interference in regard to Mr. Lumumba's movements or those of his official pursuers . . ." Yes . . . But I wanted to appeal to you personally . . . If we adhere to that policy it is Lumumba's death warrant . . . What's that? (*Laughs harshly*) Trials? Pardons? Appeals for clemency? I'm sorry, sir, but this is not Stockholm. This is the Congo. If this man falls into the hands of his enemies he will simply be slaughtered. Any protests we make will be for our own comfort — not his. Or for public relations. (*Angrily*) Yes, sir, I said public relations . . . Yes, sir, I am emotional. That is why I called you. I see my mistake now. What? Yes, of course I'll carry out the order. I'm a civil servant . . . British-trained.

(*Slams down the receiver, then takes it up again*)

Operations . . . Answer to the Ghana C.O.'s question: He is not to free Lumumba or interfere in any way — repeat — in any way . . . What? No, not if they're in battalion strength and if Lumumba is crucified before their eyes by a Congolese corporal and two men. It's an internal affair, you understand, and you know we never interfere in the internal affairs of the Congo . . . Same instructions to U.N. contingents at all airports . . .

(*Puts down telephone*)
(*Spotlight on Mobutu at microphone*)

MOBUTU

Fellow countrymen. The traitor and Communist Patrice Lumumba is in our hands. He was captured on his way to join the other traitors and Communists at Stanleyville. His capture is a shattering blow to the Communists and their accomplices

[119]

in the United Nations. He has now been brought by air to Leopoldville and has been transferred to Camp Hardy at Thysville, where he will be held in rigorous confinement until a decision is reached on how best to make him pay the full penalties for his crimes.

(*Spotlight on Kasavubu*)

KASAVUBU

I am Joseph Kasavubu, President of the Congo, acting with the approval of Joseph Mobutu. (*Reads*) The entire Free World will have learned with a sigh — with a sigh of relief of the apprehension by Congolese law'n force — law-enforcement officers of the Communist criminal Patrice Lumumba. Lumumba will soon be brought to trial, or otherwise. By order of Joseph Kasavubu by order of Joseph Mobutu.

(*On the screen the newsreel of* LUMUMBA *on arrival at Leopoldville and on transfer to Camp Hardy: without his glasses, soiled shirt, head shaven, blood clot on cheek, hands tied behind back. Spotlights on* MOBUTU *and* KASA-VUBU. *Drums off*)

MOBUTU

There is absolutely no foundation . . .

KASAVUBU

For the wild charges . . .

MOBUTU

That the criminal . . .

KASAVUBU

Communist . . .

MOBUTU

Lumumba —

KASAVUBU

On the contrary —
    (MOBUTU *looks at* KASAVUBU; KASAVUBU *looks at* MOBUTU.
They both shrug and continue)

MOBUTU

Western medical observers . . .

KASAVUBU

Conform — confirm . . .

MOBUTU

That he has been the object . . .

KASAVUBU

Of every attention . . .

MOBUTU

While Western *legal* observers . . .

KASAVUBU

Confirm — conform . . .

MOBUTU

That he will soon be brought to trial . . .

KASAVUBU

Or otherwise . . .

MOBUTU

By order of Joseph Kasavubu . . .

KASAVUBU

By order of Joseph Mobutu.

(*Spotlight on* ASDAL *at telephone*)

ASDAL

(*Cool, official*)

The transfer of Lumumba to Elisabethville has been completed, sir . . . He was observed by United Nations officers both at the take-off from Leopoldville at 1145 hours and on landing at Elisabethville at 1750 hours. He was in bad shape at take-off, and was beaten within sight of our officers; he was in much worse shape on arrival, and was again severely beaten, again under the eyes of U.N. officers and men. In both cases, of course, U.N. personnel strictly adhered to your directives, and refrained from intervention of any kind. At Elisabethville he was thrown into the back of a truck and driven off somewhere. That's all we know. What's that? *Why* did they transfer him? I don't know, sir. Oh, you wish me to speculate . . . I think they wanted him out of their hands — he is obviously a hot potato — and they didn't dare to incur the odium of murdering him here in Leopoldville where he has his friends. So they sent him to Elisabethville, where his friends have all been killed already, and where his enemies are so thirsty for his blood that they don't care what odium they incur . . . No, sir, I'm not seeking instructions; the existing instructions have been complied with and all we have to do now is to await their outcome. What's that, sir? . . . A protest or an appeal of some kind?

Quite useless, I'm afraid, sir, at this stage. "Make it for the
. . ." what's the last word, sir? . . . Oh, "record." For the
record? . . . But the record speaks for itself, don't you think,
Secretary-General?

Scene Three

20 January 1961. Morning. The Royal Palace at Laeken, near Brussels. King Baudouin, Baron d'Auge, a black page. The King is seated on something that looks like a bourgeois compromise between a throne and a chair; he wears Continental morning dress, with white tie and a decoration. He is visibly nervous and in awe of Baron d'Auge.

Baron d'Auge is in court dress, and in the beginning somewhat overplaying the part of a courtier; his demeanor should remind the audience of the earlier part of his conversation with the Monsignor in Act I. By the latter part of the scene, there is also a suggestion of sadism in the indiscreet way in which he urges his cynical view of reality on the pious young King. A smaller chair is in front of the King's chair. The page, also in uniform, is carrying a jeweled sword on a black cushion.

AUGE
(Solemnly reading)

Sire: We, the Board of Directors of the Société Universelle pour l'Amélioration de la Race Noire, et pour le Commerce, always mindful of our loyal duty to your Majesty's throne; to your Majesty personally, and to the House of Saxe-Coburg-Gotha, the imperishable line of which your Majesty inherits the glory; and mindful also of the benefits without price which your Royal House has showered upon humanity in general and upon the Société Universelle in particular; and dedicating

ourselves anew to that great task entrusted to us by your immortal predecessor (*Coughs*) Leopold II, creator of the Congo:
the task of civilization and progress in the heart of Africa;

As a mark of our loyalty, and at a solemn and auspicious
hour in the history of our civilizing mission,

Present to your Majesty through your faithful servant,
Agénor d'Auge, this Sword of Honor . . .

(*Takes the sword from the* PAGE *and presents it to the*
KING, *who takes it from him gingerly, turns it round in his
hand, partly draws it and then pushes it not quite back in
the scabbard. During this part of the scene, he should act
as if he did not know what to do with the sword, and
would like to get rid of it.* BARON D'AUGE *should show himself aware of this, but makes no move to relieve him*)

Perhaps your Majesty will permit me to remark that the
materials of which the sword is made, and its workmanship, are
entirely from the mines and factories operated by the Société
Universelle, through its subsidiaries. The iron ore for the blade
comes from our Katanga mines; the steel was forged in our
mills at Liège; the copper for the scabbard is, I need hardly
say, from Kolwezi in Katanga; the hilt is plated with platinum
from Katanga, studded with diamonds from Kasai. In brief, the
sword is symbolic of the wealth of the Congo and our exploitation of that wealth.

(*Gestures to the* PAGE, *who backs out of the royal presence. A pause.* BARON D'AUGE *looks pointedly at the empty
chair, then back at the* KING)

KING

Oh please. Please sit down, Baron. And thank you very
much . . .

[125]

AUGE

Have I your Majesty's permission to smoke? (*Lights a cigarette*) The page is also a product of the Congo, as a matter of fact. I don't know about the cushion. But I really must apologize for inflicting such an appalling speech on you, your Majesty.

KING

I thought it was rather nice . . .

AUGE

The sentiment, I agree, was admirable. But the expression! My own fault, of course. I should have read it over more carefully. One doesn't "inherit" something from something "imperishable"; one would have to wait rather a long time. And those "benefits without price"! The price of those benefits can be calculated down to the last centime. It takes a long time to calculate, I'm glad to say, but it can be done. And the bit about your immortal predecessor! If he had been immortal he could not be your predecessor. I should now be talking to Leopold II himself. What a conversation that would be!

KING

Leopold II! (*Sighs*) He sometimes worries me. He was a great man, of course. But I have read in a book that he was greedy and cruel and unkind to my great-great-aunt. Do you think that is true, Baron d'Auge?

AUGE

(*With satisfaction*)

It is true. It is even indispensable. Leopold II was greedy, unkind, cruel, like all great men. It is because he was great, that is to say excessive, in his greed and cruelty, that we today control the materials of which that sword is made up — and control also the men who win and work those materials. That is what the sword itself says, you know. A sword means the power to kill, to hurt, to frighten — and therefore the power to take. (KING *shows signs of distress*) It is the emblem of cruelty and successful greed . . . I hope your Majesty will pardon my little play of paradoxes. That is to say: I was of course joking.

KING
(*Obviously offended*)
If that were really what the sword meant, I could not possibly accept it, Baron d'Auge.

AUGE
(*Conscious that he has gone too far*)
Forgive me, your Majesty. I deeply regret my unfortunate levity; it is one of my greatest failings. Your Majesty's personal piety is an ornament of his reign, and entirely befits a constitutional monarch . . . I only meant, your Majesty, that some people think of a sword in that way. The late Einstein, for example, for that reason, refused to wear a sword, when this was expected of him for some academic ceremony in Prague. But he wasn't too squeamish to think up the Hiroshima bomb, which by the way, like your sword, was a product of our mines — *our* uranium from Shinkolobwe in Katanga. And speaking of Katanga — your Majesty will have noticed in my lamentable address a reference to "this auspicious hour"?

[127]

KING

Yes, I had wondered about that. I hadn't noticed anything particularly auspicious.

AUGE

That, your Majesty, was a delicate and perhaps rather misleading reference to a piece of information which has not yet become public, and which I sincerely hope *will* not become public. Patrice Lumumba is dead.

KING

Lumumba dead? Are you sure?

AUGE

Absolutely sure, your Majesty.

KING

How did he die?
(*His face shows growing horror during* AUGE's *narrative*)

AUGE

(*In a normal conversational tone*)

He was put to death on the evening of his arrival in Elisabethville. He was brought to the villa owned by Godefroid Munongo, Minister of the Interior of Katanga. I think your Majesty has met Godefroid Munongo?

KING

I don't know. I think so. When I was in Elisabethville I remember a big man with dark glasses who always spoke in a very low voice . . . As a matter of fact, I have had nightmares about him . . .

[128]

AUGE

Your Majesty then *has* met Godefroid Munongo . . . His
grandfather, you know, was the great M'Siri who ruled Katanga
before your Royal House acquired it in 1892. The territory was
then marked on maps simply as *Mushidi Reich*, the kingdom
of M'Siri. Your Royal House acquired the kingdom by shooting
M'Siri in his own palace, which was surrounded by a stockade,
every pole of which was surmounted by a human skull. The
energetic representative of your illustrious House brought
home M'Siri's own skull in a kerosene can. Munongo's father
then cooperated with us, in the same spirit as M'Siri himself
had cooperated with the Arab slave-traders; hating the for-
eigners but sharing in the fruits of their exploitation of his
brothers. This is the family tradition. Munongo's father got
into some trouble later with our courts. He was accused of
killing and eating a three-year-old child, in order to restore his
virility. It is said that Godefroid himself was the result of this
successful experiment. However that may be, he certainly is
immensely proud of his rather bizarre family background and
is very much the *grand seigneur*, in the African manner —
which, between ourselves, is not all that unlike the European
manner of the days when *grands seigneurs* really were *grands
seigneurs*. Munongo hates — or rather hated — Lumumba as
an upstart and demagogue who was turning the people against
their natural leaders, the chiefly families. He thus made himself
our ally against Lumumbism. He was and is a useful, though
somewhat impulsive and disquieting ally . . . It was to his
house, then, that Lumumba was brought on the evening of
seventeenth January. He had been so severely beaten that he
was unable to walk. He was propped in a chair while Munongo
bayoneted him repeatedly. He was then shot dead by one of
Munongo's assistants, a Belgian corporal. A death certificate

which did not specify the cause of death was signed by
Tshombe's doctor, another Belgian. Lumumba's body was then
disposed of in a bath of hydrochloric acid in a laboratory on
the premises of one of our subsidiary companies. No identifi-
able trace of the body remains.

KING

(*Rises to his feet in horror. The sword falls and is picked
up by* BARON D'AUGE, *who also rises. During the remainder
of the scene he holds the sword*)
What you say is abominable, Baron. If it is true, your associates are accessories to a murder!

AUGE
(*Carefully*)
I can well understand your Majesty's feelings. But the Congo
is not Brussels. The circumstances are extraordinary. A conventional jurist would no doubt describe the act as murder since
there was, of course, no form of trial. But I think the spirit of
philosophical jurisprudence would regard it in a different light
— as a kind of execution, a state execution. I think theologians
could be found who would agree to that proposition. Yes, I
could find such theologians at Louvain. Your Majesty, we do
not think of the death of Robespierre as a murder but as an
execution, though there was no trial — it was "death without
phrases," as a contemporary put it. Robespierre's crimes were
known to history and so were Lumumba's. His speech of the
thirtieth of June, that speech in which he dishonored the
Crown, was the origin of the tragedy of the Congo — the
source of all the mutinies, murders, mayhem, rape and aimless
violence that have reduced the land you ruled to chaos. Chaos
has its logic, and Lumumba's death was inscribed in that logic.

[130]

KING

(*Sitting down again*)

I shall pray for him. (AUGE *nods approvingly*) And I shall pray that his death may bring peace to the Congo.

AUGE

(*Surprised*)

Peace? To the Congo? I doubt it, your Majesty. His death was inscribed in the logic of events, but so also is bitter anger against his death. He was a very remarkable man, your Majesty, and became the object of a cult even during his life. What the announcement of his death may do we cannot predict. Our friends in Katanga, who are proud of their feat, are not likely to let it go unannounced indefinitely as they would be wise to do. We must brace ourselves against repercussions which may be formidable. We are not done with Lumumba yet, your Majesty. In fact, if I am not mistaken, Lumumba is now more dangerous than ever before. (*The* KING *sits with his face in his hands*) Have I your Majesty's permission to depart?

(*The* KING *makes no move.* AUGE *moves toward the door still carrying the sword, then turns around with a laugh*)

I almost took your sword, your Majesty. (*The* KING *looks up.* AUGE *offers him the sword. The* KING *does not take it.* AUGE *then puts the sword gently down on the seat which he himself has vacated*)

ACT FOUR

The office of the Secretary-General, on the thirty-eighth floor of the United Nations Building at Turtle Bay, East River, New York, 13 February 1961.

As the curtain rises, Diallo Diop is seated at a table left center, going through a bundle of telegrams. A large television, right center, shows on closed circuit the proceedings of the Security Council, which Hammarskjöld is addressing.

HAMMARSKJÖLD
(*On screen*)

. . . the grave and tragic news which has just reached us from Elisabethville. On this occasion I am sure I speak for all members when I express our profound regret at the news of the murder in Elisabethville of Patrice Lumumba and his companions. I should like also to express my regret at the fact that the distinguished delegate of the Soviet Union, and some other delegates, have seen fit to attribute to the United Nations some kind of responsibility for the death of Mr. Patrice Lumumba . . .

(DIOP *looks up from his telegrams at the screen. During the remainder of* HAMMARSKJÖLD's *televised remarks,* DIOP's *demeanor shows increasing signs of agitation and anger*)

. . . It was at no time in the power of the representatives of our organization to avert Mr. Lumumba's tragic fate . . .

(*Enter* BONHAM. *He looks at* DIOP, *then at the screen,*

then back at DIOP, *smiles broadly and sits on the edge of the table*)

. . . Mr. Lumumba traveled east, without any possibility for the United Nations to know where he was, and therefore without any possibility for the organization to give him protection . . .

(DIOP *rises and moves toward the screen*)

. . . He was arrested out in the country without any possibility for the United Nations to stop this action, as it was not in control of the situation . . .

(BONHAM *laughs while* DIOP *turns down the sound on the closed-circuit television.* HAMMARSKJÖLD'S *face remains visible, his lips moving, but his voice is no longer heard.* DIOP *goes back to the telegrams*)

BONHAM

Dear me . . . Your pal Jesus has just told a teeny-weeny little fib, hasn't he? How did the order go, do you remember? "To refrain from any interference with Mr. Lumumba's movements or those of his official pursuers." And now he says the United Nations had no possibility to stop the action. A little contradiction there . . . But perhaps there's a way out; perhaps, though they were under orders not to intervene, they also had in fact no possibility of intervening, or no possibility of not intervening, that is to say of refraining, by deliberate choice of their master, from intervening — if you see what I mean. No, that won't work either, will it? There were those U.N. troops on the spot at the time of arrest, who so inconveniently and indiscreetly asked for authority to intervene: that is to say that they saw a possibility of intervention and were ordered not to intervene. That clinches it, I'm afraid, even if we assume that the U.N. forces at Leopoldville airport, who witnessed Lumumba's send-off, and those at Elisabethville airport, who witnessed his arrival, were not in control of the situation — at airports which they had been able to close down at will a few months before — when it was a question of dishing Lumumba. When — come to think of it — it was *already* a question of dishing Lumumba. Those who prevented him from flying of his own accord were not inconsistent in allowing him to be flown off by those official pursuers — a nice phrase. And Hammarskjöld can't pretend either, as he did in September, that he simply doesn't know what was done. Lumumba was arrested more than two months ago and consigned to Elisabethville for disposal a little less than a month ago. Hammarskjöld must know all the details by now. No, there's no way round it: that solemn little noise we have just heard was the distinctive note of a Secretary-General lying to a Security Council. Which presumably is why you turned it off. Right, Diop?

(DIOP, *without replying, continues to open, read and sort telegrams*)

Oh, well, let's have a look at the fan mail. (*He takes up the nearest bunch of telegrams and begins to read*) "Hideous crime" . . . "monstrous crime" . . . "heinous crime" . . . "odious scandal" . . . "blood on your hands" . . . "imperialist stooge" . . . "assassin" . . . "resign" . . . "betrayal of your trust" . . . "resign" — again . . . "assassin" — again. These are hardly rave notices, are they? And the names of the reviewers make it a lot worse: Ghana, Guinea, Mali, Egypt, the wild ones were to be expected; but Nigeria, Liberia, Tunisia, Ethiopia as well, the respectable pro-Western lot . . . The boss is really in trouble.

(HAMMARSKJÖLD's *face disappears from the screen and is*

replaced by that of ADLAI STEVENSON. DIOP *and* BONHAM
look at the screen. DIOP *rises to switch on the sound.*
BONHAM *continues*)

Yes, we'd better listen to Stevenson . . . His Master's Voice.

STEVENSON
(*On screen*)

. . . the first occasion for the United States under the leader-
ship of President Kennedy to speak formally in the Security
Council on a question of substance. I should like to add my
voice to those of other members of the Council who have expressed our profound regret and sense of shock at the news of
the tragic death of Mr. Lumumba and at other acts of violence
in the Congo. At the same time I must deplore the unfounded
charges which have so recklessly been hurled at our organization. Yes, *at our organization* for the malicious attacks directed
against our Secretary-General — by people who have not hesi-
tated to stoop so low as to ascribe to him actual responsibility
for the death of Mr. Lumumba — these attacks are really attacks on the United Nations itself, through the Secretary-General. So that the issue before us is not one of personalities —
has nothing to do with whatever opinions we may hold or have
held of Mr. Lumumba or of Mr. Hammarskjöld as men. No, the
simple and momentous issue before us is that of the future of
the United Nations. Are we callously to cast aside the one instrument that men have developed to safeguard their peace
and security? Are we to abandon the jungles of the Congo . . .

(*A scream is heard over the television sound track. A
voice, momentarily drowning* MR. STEVENSON'S: "*Get out!
Get out! Get out of the Congo!*")

STEVENSON

(Continuing against rising background noise suggestive of shouts and crashes)

Are we to abandon the jungles of the Congo to the jungles of internecine warfare and of international rivalry? The issue then is simply this: shall the United Nations survive?

(The speaker's voice is drowned by the rising clamor, in which only a few remarks can be distinguished)

A VOICE

(Shouting, in distance)

Murderer!

ANOTHER VOICE

(Whispering near microphone)

Clear the gallery, for Christ's sake!

(The screen goes blank; the sound track continues)

SHOUTING VOICE

You killed him! You crucified him!

ENGLISH VOICE

The President of the Council directs that the public gallery be immediately cleared and suspends the session until this is done . . .

(Confused noise continues from the blank screen. BONHAM *turns down the sound track)*

BONHAM

(Thoughtfully)

The telegrams take shape . . . and voice . . . Spontaneous

outburst of African indignation? Hardly. Who would pay all those fares? Afro-American indignation? What do they know about the Congo or Lumumba? Or is it quite simply a Communist stunt, Diop? What do you think?

DIOP

(*Fiercely, mimicking*)

Afro-American indignation! Bonham, your stinking little mind is all choked up with the kind of snot that runs out of the editorials you read. You can't even *hear* any more! That noise there wasn't anything nice and abstract like Communism. It was hate, Bonham, black hate. It was the noise of people who would like to cut the throats of people like you. As I would cut yours, if I could get away with it, and go on to cut some more like it. There are plenty of them.

(STEVENSON's *face appears again on the television screen.* BONHAM, *smiling pleasantly, turns up the sound*)

STEVENSON

(*On screen*)

May I say that I deeply deplore this outrageous and obviously organized demonstration that has just taken place. To the extent that Americans may be involved, I apologize . . .

(DIOP *howls and starts to lift up the television set, as if about to throw it on the floor*)

STEVENSON

. . . on behalf of my Government to the members of the Security Council.

(BONHAM *reaches past* DIOP *and switches off the television.* DIOP *stares in a dazed way at the blank and silent screen, then gently replaces the set*)

BONHAM

That's better. No good smashing the set just because you dislike the man in the picture. Smash the man if you can, and if you can't, just shut up until you can. And shut up then, too. Or better still, express your "profound regret" at the tragic smashing of the man you smashed. You'll learn, Diop, in time. You're well placed for it . . .

DIOP

(*To himself, in a sort of trance of rage*)

The jungles of the Congo! The jungles of the Congo! Oh! The bastard, the shit! And that apology . . . (*Mimicking a Southern gentlemen*) "To the extent that mah nigguhs may have been involved, suh, in eatin' watamelons on yo' plantation, Ah begs to tendah, suh, mah apologies for mah nigguhs —fo' which of course Ah take full responsibility to yo' and to yo' gracious lady."

BONHAM

Some watermelons! I bet some skulls got cracked in this one. In any case, I get the point. All this is an outburst of genuine African indignation. And you as a genuine African share this indignation. Good. But there's just one thing I don't quite understand. Hammarskjöld is, let's say, your boss. Lumumba was certainly your hero. Now your boss has bumped off your hero. Good. So what do you, a genuinely indignant African, actually do? Do you kill your boss? No. Do you commit suicide? No. Do you even resign? No. You sit here. You mumble abuse of Mr. Stevenson, and you are rude to your more unashamedly Caucasian colleagues, like myself. But you stay on, Diop. You sort your telegrams. And you draw your pay? How come? I wonder what happened between the pair of you when the news of Lumumba's murder broke? Did you have some kind of little tiff? And did you kiss and make up? And shed a tear, together, in memory of poor, dear Patrice?

DIOP
(*Impassively*)
I am here because there is unfinished business to be attended to. The nature of the business you and your friends will learn in due course.
(*A pause*)

BONHAM
I think I take your meaning. *Delenda est Katanga,* is that it?
(*No reply*)
The idea, then would be to complete Lumumba's task by taking advantage of the indignation aroused by his death in order to mount a U.N. operation against Katanga. Reunification of the Congo by force. Occupation of the capital in which Lumumba was murdered. Expropriation of the financial interests behind his murder. Ethiopian troops in the smelter of the Société Universelle. Triumph of African nationalism: tableau. Very attractive I'm sure, for those who like that sort of thing. Also very risky. Katanga is not without resources. And not without friends — some of whom are quite impulsive as of course you know by now. But perhaps that is part of the attraction, even part of the scenario: Boy has hero. Boy also has boss. Boss consents to murder of hero. Boy pushes boss into avenging hero. Boss avenges hero and is killed in so doing. Boy laughs like drain. Too complicated perhaps? But something like that is implicit in the situation, don't you think? (*In a more excited tone*) You know, politically, all this is terrible nonsense, but

aesthetically I must confess it has a certain traditional atavistic appeal — which you of course must feel quite strongly . . .

(*Enter* HAMMARSKJÖLD, *who stands unnoticed at the door during* BONHAM's *peroration*)

The idea of Lumumba's ghost, more powerful than the living man, raining death and destruction on all his adversaries! It's pure Shakespeare.

(*Raising his arms, and slowly pivoting while he loudly declaims*)

"And Caesar's spirit, ranging for revenge, . . . Shall in these confines with a monarch's voice Cry —"

HAMMARSKJÖLD

. . . "Havoc and let slip the dogs of war"! That's what he cries, is it not?

(HAMMARSKJÖLD's *demeanor is perceptibly different from that in Act II. His hair, sleeked down in Act II, is now rather rumpled and standing up. He moves and speaks with greater energy and decision, and a hint of exaltation*)

If the dramatic performance is finished, Bonham, I have a job for you. It has to do with the latest onset of havoc inside this building. Some of the rioters are in custody, some of them are hurt and some of the security guards are pretty badly hurt. The women in the gallery were mourning their Lumumba with the aid of those stiletto heels . . . I want you to talk to the police. That's something you're rather good at. Get as many of the rioters out of jail as you can. We're not pressing charges, of course. Just get them out. The American Delegation will help you if you need help.

BONHAM

Yes, sir. (*He moves to leave*)

HAMMARSKJÖLD

Oh, and Bonham . . . (BONHAM *stops*) The press will be around. Be very careful what you say to them. No "appalling," no "outrageous." And no sneers, Bonham, no sneers at all. This is not the moment to remind the public how civilized you are — and how white. The demonstrators were seriously misled, but we understand their genuine indignation and their anxiety that the conditions in the Congo which led to the murder of Patrice Lumumba should be speedily corrected. That's the note. Repeat: that the conditions in the Congo which led to the murder of Patrice Lumumba should be speedily corrected. It's important to use precisely that wording. Have you got it?

BONHAM

Yes, sir . . .

HAMMARSKJÖLD

You look surprised, Bonham. It's curious how surprised people are when something they say turns out to be true. Cultivate your feeling for poetry, Bonham. It's genuine and may save you yet. What Shakespeare told you is true. Caesar's spirit *is* ranging for revenge and this is the hour of Caesar's spirit. In these days of course and in this place especially, havoc is not exactly cried; the noise is more like a whisper: "Conditions exist . . . which should be speedily corrected." Very gently and with an emphasis on the sibilants. You can hardly hear the dogs being slipped, but already they are moving . . . You don't like this part, do you, Bonham?

BONHAM

No, sir, quite frankly I don't. And if I may . . .

[144]

HAMMARSKJÖLD

No, Bonham, you may not. You have become politically inaudible — just as poor Diallo was politically inaudible before.
You see, then, I was deaf in my left ear, my black ear; now I
must be deaf in my right ear for a while. The white one. Please
go now, and do what you have to do.

(*Exit* BONHAM)

DIOP

(*Businesslike*)

Do you want to look at the telegrams?

HAMMARSKJÖLD

I know what's in them generally. I've been listening to the
African delegates. Is there anything particularly interesting?

DIOP

There's one from the President of Guinea.

HAMMARSKJÖLD

What does Sekou Touré say?

DIOP

(*Reads, in a flat voice*)

"This sorry drama in which you took a predominant part
despite your repeated protestations dishonors you personally
in the eyes of the embittered public of Africa and the world.
Now that the curtain has fallen on the first act of your criminal
tragedy, it is essential that you draw the lesson of universal
condemnation from this crime."

HAMMARSKJÖLD

Curious, isn't it, that people as different as Bonham and Touré have to think in dramatic terms about this. And the people in the gallery just now when they hissed the villain . . . Do you agree with Sekou Touré, Diallo? That I am . . . personally dishonored?

DIOP

(*Hard*)

What do you think yourself? When you hear yourself saying there was no possibility to intervene? When you know that it is not true?

HAMMARSKJÖLD

(*Gravely*)

My honor is intact and unsullied because I did what I had to do for the high purpose to which I have dedicated my life, and for that high purpose only. My personal honor consists of the service of this organization and of world peace, and has no separate existence from that. If it is necessary to lie in the cause of peace, then I will lie. And do so without loss of honor, because the soul of honor is integrity of purpose.

DIOP

Service of peace? I must say you have some pretty rough ways of serving peace . . . A few lies, a little bribery. A murder here and there . . . And by the way, is it in the service of peace that you're now letting slip those dogs of war? *I* approve of the use of force against the foreign troops in Katanga — that's why I'm still here — but *I* don't wear a halo and preach about peace . . .

HAMMARSKJÖLD

I have no use for moralists who can't count. Or for pacifists who are prepared to let the world blow up, provided they can keep their boring little consciences clean. The purpose of this strange institution in which we work is the greatest purpose humanly imaginable. It is nothing less than to save the human species from thermonuclear self-destruction. If that task requires some dirty work, I am prepared to get my hands dirty and even bloody. If it requires the death of Patrice Lumumba, I vote for the death of Patrice Lumumba. If it requires lying about the death of Patrice Lumumba, I lie about that death. And if it requires the extinction by force of the Independent State of Katanga, then I will extinguish Katanga by force . . . and by the way, Diallo, it's no use trying to make me ashamed of my halo. In this office a halo is what the sociologists call *eufunctional,* that is to say it works. So I'm glad that I happen to have a halo, which is visible for a considerable distance.

DIOP
(*Smiling for the first time*)
It's not so visible close up.

HAMMARSKJÖLD
(*Also smiling*)
And I'm glad of that, too. But seriously, I'm sorry, Diallo, that you lack the religious imagination . . .

DIOP
(*Still derisive, but more gently*)
If I had it what would I imagine, like?

HAMMARSKJÖLD

You would not imagine. You are imagining now. You would see Abraham sacrificing Isaac. You would see what Kierkegaard called the teleological suspension of the ethical —

DIOP

(*Amazed*)

You are Abraham? And Lumumba is Isaac?

HAMMARSKJÖLD

I am a figure of Abraham; Lumumba a figure of Isaac. And Isaac, you know, is also Jesus. The sacrifice in Elisabethville is also the sacrifice on Calvary: Gethsemane was in Thysville. Leon Bloy said that the face of any man becomes, at the moment it is struck, the face of Jesus. And it is through the death of Lumumba that mankind at this time comprehends the Crucifixion. That is why the women are crying.

DIOP

You look a bit like Pontius Pilate to me.

HAMMARSKJÖLD

Undoubtedly. Pilate was an instrument of God's will, like Abraham's knife. But Pilate was a skeptic like you. I, being a religious man, have some glimmering of God's purposes, being accomplished through me. And in one life the same man, having played the part of Pilate may be called to play the part of Jesus. Playing parts again, you see in a Divine Comedy. That is why this thing here exists — this United Nations — this gadget, as de Gaulle called it. The gadget has a more precise name . . . it is called a stage. It is a stage for the continuous dramatization of world history — for the interrogation of his-

tory by the moral and religious sense. It is the scene for the
Passion Play of human destiny.

DIOP

I don't get it. I mean the practical application, which I suppose lurks somewhere in all mysteries. Is it that the blood of
the martyrs is the seed of the Church? Lumumba being the
martyr and the United Nations the Church?

HAMMARSKJÖLD

A martyr. There have been others, and there will be still
more. Of course the United Nations is the Church, the com-
munion of mankind. That which is worthy to be served, in the
purpose of God, will always be the Church. However unlikely
it may appear.

DIOP

And you're the Pope?

HAMMARSKJÖLD

Yes. I am the Vicar of Christ. I look like Pontius Pilate. But
I represent Christ. My service in this Church can have no other
meaning. History — as Bloy also said — is the March of God
in darkness. In that dark march I take care never to let go of
my Father's hand. *Nec patris linquens dexteram* . . .

DIOP

Jesus! Dag, you're out of your mind!

HAMMARSKJÖLD
(*Smiling*)

I know, Diallo . . . You have to go out of your mind, you
know, in order to get into your soul.

(*Enter* SENHORA GATTABLANCA. *She is agitated, and has apparently been crying*)

SRA. GATTABLANCA

I'm sorry to interrupt, Secretary-General, but it's important
. . . among the demonstrators in the gallery there was a young
woman . . . a certain Madame Rose Rose . . . she was Lumumba's secretary and, they say, his mistress . . . *she* says she
was his junior wife . . . she was one of the most violent of the
rioters — smashed a guard's face with the heel of her shoe. She
was hurt too and she seems somehow not quite right . . . If
the press see her, it will be more . . . more scandal . . . and
she wants to see you.

HAMMARSKJÖLD
(*Softly*)

Does she, Carmen, does she? Very well, please bring her
here. (*As* SRA. GATTABLANCA *moves to leave*) Carmen! You
admired Patrice Lumumba didn't you?

SRA. GATTABLANCA
(*Sadly*)

Yes, I did . . .

HAMMARSKJÖLD

And you were horrified by the circumstances of his death?

SRA. GATTABLANCA

I have not been able to sleep since I heard the news.

HAMMARSKJÖLD

So what do you think of me?

SRA. GATTABLANCA
(*Slowly*)

I cannot think of you at all, because the person I thought of
as you does not seem to be there. For me you were the good
man. And that is why I cannot sleep. Not for the loss of Lumumba but for the loss of you. For the loss of the good
man . . .

HAMMARSKJÖLD
(*Calmly*)

Be sad, Carmen, but not too sad. The good man is always
there. But he is not always the same man. Please bring me
Madame Rose.

(*Exit* SRA. GATTABLANCA)

DIOP

Do you know her?

HAMMARSKJÖLD

Madame Rose? I have spoken to her. Or to what was her,
then. Her lover was alive, and she was happy.

(*Enter* MADAME ROSE. *She has a black eye and her left
arm is in a sling. Her face is bruised and scratched and
rather flushed. Her clothes are shabby and torn. She seems
a little drunk, especially in the early part of the scene. She
is almost unrecognizable as from her previous appearance.*
HAMMARSKJÖLD *puts out his hand. After a moment's hesita-
tion she takes it briefly, then draws her hand back*)

MADAME ROSE
(*Almost as if talking in her sleep*)

I wanted to feel what it was like. It's not that I wondered
whether you were human. I wondered whether you were even

[151]

a mammal. I thought your hand would not be like us. More like a bird perhaps. Or a snake . . .

HAMMARSKJÖLD

(*Intently*)

And was it? What did you feel?

MADAME ROSE

That's what's so funny. It wasn't cold. It was hot. Like a fever. I never thought it would be like that. Maybe all the cold has gone into your mind . . . I can't understand it at all. Patrice is cold now, and you are warm. That's not how it should be, is it? It should be the other way round. *You* were the cold one, always thinking of things, and analyzing and correcting and calling on the telephone to tell people they were dead, and to explain exactly why. Do you remember talking to me on the telephone?

HAMMARSKJÖLD

I remember.

MADAME ROSE

Why don't you say it?

HAMMARSKJÖLD

Say what?

MADAME ROSE

That if he had listened to you he would be alive today.

HAMMARSKJÖLD

There would be no use in saying that now. It would only cause you pain.

[152]

MADAME ROSE

That's right. And you shouldn't cause pain, should you? Except in the cause of algebra. If it's for algebra it's all right to stab a man and drive his woman mad. But Patrice couldn't do your kind of algebra. Can you believe that? That's really why he couldn't listen to you, you know. You talk equations all the time, and he couldn't do those ones. What he could do was dancing, and making love, and talking to Congolese people, and drinking and saying silly things that made people laugh, and waving a sword and imagining he was Prime Minister of the Congo . . . While all the time he was just the bit in the equation that you cancel out — in order to get your solution, you see. He said you had no balls, you know, and he seemed to think that was very important. But he was wrong, of course, because you don't need balls to do algebra. And that's what cancels out *his*.

(*Notices* DIOP *for the first time and addresses him*)
You're black!

DIOP

(*Gently*)
I am black, Madame Rose.

MADAME ROSE

Then what are you doing here? Are you a traitor?

DIOP

No, Madame Rose. I was for Patrice Lumumba. I am against his murderers.

MADAME ROSE

Against his murderers? And sitting here with Dag Hammar-

[153]

skjöld? Well, thank God for a laugh. Tell me, are you his black
boy friend that they talk about?

DIOP

(*Staring at* MADAME ROSE; *in an absentminded tone, as
if her question was of little importance in comparison with
her appearance*)
That's what they say.

MADAME ROSE
(*Mimics*)
"That's what they say," is it? Listen — I was Lumumba's
girl friend and I didn't find out that I was by reading the news-
paper or listening to the radio. It was, kind of, more a personal
matter. It was — until this Swedish contraption that you don't
know whether it's your boy friend or not calculated us both
out of existence. What the hell *are* you doing here anyway?

DIOP
(*In distress*)
I . . . it's for Lumumba's sake. It's the same cause. They're
going to have to free the Congo now. To break Katanga. Just
because of Lumumba. Because of Lumumba's death.
(*He is on the verge of breaking down*)

HAMMARSKJÖLD
I think I can explain . . .

MADAME ROSE
Yes, that's what you think you can do, all right. But not to
me. Explain yourself to what you haven't got. And do it
quietly. (*To* DIOP) What's your name?

[154]

DIOP
Diop — Diallo Diop.

MADAME ROSE

Well, *be* Diallo Diop. Don't be a letter in one of *his* equations, and get yourself canceled out . . . you're a nice-looking boy, Diallo . . . a decent African boy. This is no place for you . . . stop crying and stand up. (*He stands up*) Look at my face. (*He looks at her*) This is the face of the junior widow of Patrice Lumumba. It used to be a pretty face; it's a bit knocked about now. Kiss me, Diallo! (DIOP *hesitates*) Kiss me! Hard! At once! (*He kisses her; she responds ardently.* HAMMARSKJÖLD *looks on impassively*) All right . . . I'm taking you out of this snake pit. We'll go back to Africa, to Stanleyville, and if we get killed, at least we'll be killed among people we like. And if people ask you whether you're Lumumba's junior widow's boy friend you won't have to say, "that's what they say." You'll bloody well *know*. (*To* HAMMARSKJÖLD) Well, your Majesty. How do you like the cursing widow scene?

HAMMARSKJÖLD
(*Still calm*)
I had been expecting it, Madame Rose.

MADAME ROSE
Of course. Duly allowed for in the calculations, and appropriately discounted. Well, it's nearly over now, and with it your love affair. Or whatever it was. And after all, you'll still be able to write and explain and enjoy yourself in your own way. Come on, Diallo Diop.
(*Yanks* DIOP *by the wrist*)

[155]

DIOP

(*Gently disengages himself*)

I'm sorry, Madame Rose. I'm on your side — Lumumba's side. And that's why I'm going to stay. There's nothing I could do in Stanleyville that others can't do. It's here that I'm needed.

(MADAME ROSE *laughs unsteadily*)

Oh, forget that. There is a task to be completed, what Lumumba had begun, the destruction of Katanga and all that it stands for; the reunification of the Congo. Until that is accomplished . . .

MADAME ROSE

(*Weary and in shock*)

Oh, you poor fish, what a lot of crap. Your pal here just works for the Yanks. He helped them kill Patrice. *He* won't finish what Patrice began. He'll finish what he began himself. He'll give the Congo to the Yanks. And you're going to help him, you poor dumb black! Well, to hell with you. (*To* HAMMAR-SKJÖLD) All right, so you keep him. One more nigger you've made a monkey of. (*Grips him by the lapel*) Is it true that you think you're God?

HAMMARSKJÖLD

(*Steadily*)

I am a servant of God. And I accept what comes to me in God's service.

MADAME ROSE

It must be a comfort to think you're serving God when you have to murder a man by remote control. (*Moving back a little, still holding his lapel, in a louder voice*) All right, Jesus, this is the bit where you get spat on. (*Spits in his face.* DIOP,

[156]

terrified, moves toward HAMMARSKJÖLD, *but* MADAME ROSE
stands between them facing DIOP, *and addresses him*) I am
Patrice Lumumba's junior widow. (*She breaks down.* DIOP
*puts his arm around her shoulder and guides her out of the
room.* HAMMARSKJÖLD *takes out a handkerchief and carefully
wipes the spit off his face*)
(*Enter a* SENIOR AIDE, *carrying papers*)

SENIOR AIDE

I met young Diop in the corridor with a woman who looked
as if she'd just escaped from a lunatic asylum. What's going on?

HAMMARSKJÖLD

Just another casualty of peace preservation . . . not the first
or the last . . . she was Lumumba's girl . . . she upset Diop
pretty badly.

SENIOR AIDE

Lumumba's girl . . . more fuel for the mob if the press gets
hold of that story.

HAMMARSKJÖLD

Quite so. And that may be just what we need in the present
conjuncture.

SENIOR AIDE
(*Reflectively*)

Oh, I see . . . Do you want to discuss these names for the
post of your representative in Elisabethville?

HAMMARSKJÖLD

In a moment. You've been talking to the American Delegation, I expect . . . how does it look from there?

SENIOR AIDE

Pretty bad. Or good, depending on the point of view. The timing of this announcement was extraordinarily inept. The new Administration in Washington wants to woo the new African states, acquire a new, positive image and all that, and now all they hear is howls of execration. They're very anxious to recover popularity and influence in Africa. And they are very anxious that the United Nations — and you personally — should recover popularity and influence in Africa.

HAMMARSKJÖLD

And how do they think they, and we, can do that?

SENIOR AIDE

(*Reluctantly*)

You know the answer. Heavy pressure on Katanga. Reunification of the Congo. Definitive proof that the United States and the United Nations are the friends of Africa. There's a draft resolution calling for the use of force if necessary in the last resort. The United States will vote in favor.

HAMMARSKJÖLD

Leaving me to judge when the last resort is reached, and when force is necessary?

SENIOR AIDE

Yes.

HAMMARSKJÖLD

And, apart from voting for resolutions, what will happen when it comes to the point? If we have to use force, will they back us up?

[158]

limits. I know of course that there is something fictitious both about the new states and about the United Nations. But under the fiction again there is something real. It is a kind of parable . . .

(*The* AIDE *moves restlessly.* HAMMARSKJÖLD *smiles*)

I'm sorry! It boils down to this: with the assurance of a necessary minimum of U.S. support, I am going to treat the new resolution seriously. I am going to put real pressure on Katanga to abandon secession, and if they won't, or their backers won't, then force will be used . . . In the last resort . . . Now let's look at these curricula of yours.

(*Glances through papers handed to him by the* AIDE. *Tosses most of them aside and holds one*)

Any of these people would be fine, if I were going to take your advice. But as I'm not, there's only this one. What about him?

(*Hands the paper to the* AIDE, *who looks at it and grunts*)

SENIOR AIDE

Yes, I was afraid you'd take that one. You know him yourself, I think.

HAMMARSKJÖLD

I've met him. I've read a book of his, as a matter of fact. Curiously enough, it was sent to me from Sweden by an old enemy of mine. I've often wondered why. Not a bad book; some interesting things in it about Leon Bloy . . .

SENIOR AIDE
(*Puzzled*)
The French Prime Minister?

[161]

HAMMARSKJÖLD

No Andy, not the French Prime Minister . . . In any case, I'm curious to know what you think about this man yourself.

SENIOR AIDE

He's a trouble-maker, if that's what you want. Clever. Bumptious. Talks too much. The British say he's a Communist, but they just mean that he's Irish. He likes to hobnob with Africans and Asians, and behaves a bit like one. He would just love himself as a kind of anti-imperialist proconsul. In short, he's the very man to send to Katanga if you want all hell to break loose.

HAMMARSKJÖLD

(*Quietly*)

Yes. I'm going to send him there because that's where all hell *has* to break loose at this moment. If it's not to break loose elsewhere on a much greater scale. Go send for him — and tell him to get ready to leave for Elisabethville.

ACT FIVE

Scene One

29 August 1961. *The board room of Conceded Concessions, Ltd., in London. Duke of Tamworth, Sir Henry Large-White, Baron d'Auge.*

AUGE

So you see, gentlemen, we are in presence of a new situation. The old assumption that the United Nations would talk forever, and do nothing, no longer holds. They have by their surprise action of yesterday expelled most of the so-called mercenaries, who were of course regular officers in the Belgian Army. The result is that the State of Katanga, which we have hitherto regarded as the shield of our interests, is now exposed to serious risk. The question we have to decide — quite urgently — is the direction in which we should use our influence. Should we drop our support for the secession and defend our interests by other means — by aligning our policy with that of the present American Administration, cooperating fully with the United Nations, and generally cultivating a new image in accordance with the spirit of the age? Or should we encourage resistance to the United Nations by means of guerrilla war and terrorism. Either path, as usual, involves certain risks . . .

LARGE-WHITE

I shouldn't have thought there was much doubt about where the greater risk lies. Capitulation in Katanga means in practice

[165]

leaving it to the Americans to protect our interests. And they won't do it. They'll protect their own damned image at the cost of our interests and to the benefit of theirs. They'll let the Africans get nominal control over the resources which we own, and as they will have real control over the Africans — as they have already in Leopoldville — *they* will control the resources too. And what goes for Katanga will go for the copper belt and the rest of Rhodesia. And other places. All this pious talk you hear from the Yanks about African nationalism simply means they like the idea of using black catspaws to seize our property for them. Well, I'm for not letting them. And I'm for whatever has to be done in order not to let them. Whatever has to be done . . .

TAMWORTH
(*Laughs*)

Good, fiery stuff, Harry. The only problem is whether we can get away with it. It's very tricky ground. You remember there were people who thought that everything would be splendid once Lumumba was out of the way. I think you were one of those, Harry. But it didn't work out that way. We didn't get the sword back; we haven't yet got it back; and I doubt if we ever will. Personally, I'm inclined to accept the fact that we've come down in the world. I think I should be content to play a minor part in the American Way of Life. An amiable sort of character part; the title will do no harm at all. (*Laughter. To* AUGE) Well, Agénor, what do you think?

AUGE

I think Harry is right about what happens to us if we capitu-

late. I think *you* are right about the serious risks if we choose
to fight. But on the whole I favor a fight. There is a reasonable
chance of winning. How good it is no one can assess. A mixed
United Nations force is a sort of fabulous animal; nobody yet
knows how it can fight, or whether it can fight. Personally, I
think there is a good chance that it would become afflicted by
diplomatic convulsions, once the fighting started. It is, after all,
a rather vague sort of coalition founded on various pretenses,
and on unrealistic assumptions about human nature. A coalition, moreover, led by a sort of saint. Hammarskjöld at the
moment seems to be driven on by guilt over the death of Lumumba. It is not a motive power which could take him very far
without American permission, of course. But there are signs
that he has taken that permission to go just a little further than
they expected him to go. If we capitulate, this becomes a triumph for him. But if we encourage armed resistance, then
either he draws back — which is excellent, of course — or he
has to plunge forward, alarming his most essential backers, and
perhaps being restrained by them. We could expect some
diplomatic help, at this stage, from your country, Beowulf.
Also, a saint driven by guilt is an unpredictable sort of machine.
Perhaps by making him guilty about blood shed in Elisabethville we can actually put him into reverse? But in any case,
even if this does not work, we should be little worse off than if
Katanga capitulated without a fight. We should, of course, dis-
claim all responsibility for what would be nominally acts
resulting from the spontaneous indignation of the black
Katangese at being separated from their beloved Belgian officers. In short, serious possibilities of substantial gain, relatively small risks of greater loss. In substance, I am of Harry's
opinion: for resistance.

TAMWORTH

Very well, but do the material possibilities for such resistance exist — after the expulsion of the Belgian officers?

AUGE

Not if it were a question of inflicting military defeat on the U.N. forces. But it is a question of defeating them psychologically and diplomatically. That is within our possibilities. It is for that reason that I have brought here this evening a French officer, Colonel Alcibiade Zbyre, who describes himself as a specialist in subversive warfare. I have brought Colonel Zbyre here for two reasons: first in order that you may hear his assessment of what can be done on the spot, and second so that you may know the type of men we have to call to our aid. He is, frankly, not a reassuring personality. But, then, our situation is not one in which a reassuring personality would be of much use to us. May I introduce him?

(*As* TAMWORTH *nods,* AUGE *rings a bell. An* USHER *appears*)

Colonel Zbyre, please . . .

(*Exit* USHER)

His English is not very good, I'm afraid, but his impact is essentially nonverbal.

(*Enter* COLONEL ZBYRE, *a large man in black civilian clothes with a shaven skull, a black patch over one eye and leather gloves which he does not remove*)

Colonel Zbyre . . . the Duke of Tamworth, Sir Harry Large-White.

(ZBYRE *clicks his heels and bows; the others nod*)

Please sit down, Colonel.

(*The* COLONEL *sits*)

My colleagues have substantial investments in the Congo,

Colonel, and they would like to know your assessment of the current situation there. First of all, what exactly was the nature of your own duties there?

ZBYRE

Essentially I am intellectual.

AUGE

Yes?

ZBYRE

Duties of intellectual are those of logic, is it not?

TAMWORTH

Perhaps, Colonel Zbyre, in somewhat more concrete terms . . .

ZBYRE

Ah, the Englishmen appreciate the candor! So. Essessination — that is morder. Interrogation — that is torture. There is also the embuscade. And kidnipping, for which are required specialists. All is in the logic of situation. But is expensive.

AUGE

You will understand, Colonel, that the details of your work are not our concern here. My colleagues and I know nothing of political affairs.

(ZBYRE *laughs heartily*)

But we are, of course, concerned — in a general way — with peace, order and good government in the areas where our investments lie.

ZBYRE
(*Chuckles*)
Very good. Is English for to fight or not to fight?

AUGE
(*Smiling*)
Suppose the Katanga authorities were to decide to resist the United Nations —

ZBYRE
(*Violently*)
The United Nations are all Kents!

TAMWORTH
Kents?

AUGE
Ce sont tous des cons?

ZBYRE
Naturellement.

AUGE
He means, gentlemen, that he has a low opinion of the virility and fighting spirit of the U.N. forces . . .

ZBYRE
They are not intellectual. They are Indians, Irish, Swedes. So they can be defeated by intellectual warfare.

AUGE
How?

ZBYRE

First you bit pipple.

TAMWORTH

Bit pipple?

AUGE

Beat people . . .

ZBYRE

Or rather you pay black pipple to bit other black pipple, then you ask United Nations where is order? And you go on bitting pipple and asking them where is order and bitting harder and asking louder till they do *something*. (*Bangs the table*) And when they do something you shoot at them from the houses and when they shoot back at the houses you take pictures and ask them where is order, what is U.N. doing? Above all, you gentlemen will not hesitate to use pepper.

LARGE-WHITE

Pepper?

AUGE

Paper. He is referring to what he regards as our influence over media of public opinion.

ZBYRE

Yes. Pepper and reddio. In London, Washington, New York, Paris, Brussels. The barbarities of the U.N.! The essessinations! The tortures! The kidnippings! The bittings! The reppings, the nuns, the prists and the ocular witnesses. And so on as long as necessity. All the good souls that love the U.N. get sick to their stomachs, and make love to peace some more. So compromise solution — It can be done but is expensive.

AUGE

Thank you, Colonel. Very interesting. You do understand, don't you, that our sole interest in this matter is the normal concern of property owners for peace and order in the territory. In Katanga, when you return you will no doubt be in touch with our local managers about security arrangements in the area of our installations. I am sure mutually satisfactory arrangements can be worked out.

ZBYRE

(*Rising*)

Between intellectuals we understand one another at half-word. Is in logic of situation. Good evening, gentlemen.

(*Exit* ZBYRE)

TAMWORTH

I often wondered what a French intellectual was like . . .

LARGE-WHITE

Good God! Exit First Murderer! Agénor, old man, do you really have to bring in people like that?

AUGE

(*Softly*)

You brought him in, you know, when you said "'whatever has to be done." He's Mr. Whatever, and I thought you'd better see him. We can, of course, vote for "whatever" without wanting to know what it is. Or who he is. But in this case I thought you'd better see him. Myself, I think we have to use

[172]

him. But there's no use pretending there aren't some risks involved . . . Having seen him, are you still of the same opinion
— for "whatever has to be done"?

LARGE-WHITE

I'm still of the same opinion, of course. And you know the
local situation. I'd be happy to leave it up to you, really. But I
really wish you wouldn't bring characters like that around here.
Enough to put a man off his dinner. Almost.

TAMWORTH

Well, you two must do as you think best. I'm sure you understand the whole situation much better than I do. But I want no
part of it. As they say. And I vote to meet no more of your Mr.
Whatevers, Agénor, I'll take the rest on trust. I never liked
French intellectuals much at the best of times, but that's the
fishiest specimen I ever saw. I don't want to hear any more
about the whole business.

AUGE

I assure you, your wishes will be respected. But it will be essential that your very considerable international influence
should be brought to bear at the proper moment . . .

TAMWORTH

Oh, I'll try to stop Dag from making a fool of himself, if
that's what you mean. And there's nothing immoral in working
for a compromise peace. I hope. Well, sufficient unto the day
. . . or is that quite what I mean . . .
                    (*Rises, as do the others*)
You're coming with me, Harry, aren't you? Agénor, I expect
you'll be busy with "whatever has to be done." Remember, I
don't want to hear about it.

[173]

Scene Two

September 1961. In the center of the stage a radio. Upstage a placard reading "London," a placard "Leopoldville" with table and telephone left, a placard "Elisabethville" with table and telephone right; downstage a placard "Ndola." Near it a chair, table and telephone. Between Ndola and Elisabethville a white line with the word "Rhodesia" on the Ndola side and "Katanga" on the Elisabethville side.

A U.N. soldier stands on the Katanga side of the white line. When the curtain rises, Tamworth and Auge are seated beside the placard "London." Tshombe and the British Consul, Munongo and Colonel Zbyre form two groups seated beside the placard "Elisabethville." Hammarskjöld alone is standing beside the placard "Leopoldville." At "Ndola" the stage is empty, except for an armchair. At right center a map of the Congo and adjacent part of Rhodesia showing positions of Leopoldville, Elisabethville and Ndola. From the right-hand side of the stage drumming is heard continuously, punctuated from time to time by the noise of rifle, machine-gun and mortar firing.

RADIO

(Fast)

At 4 A.M. this morning in Elisabethville, Katanga, United Nations Forces occupied the post office, radio station, and other public buildings, which were defended by Katangese forces.

The United Nations representative in Elisabethville declared
the secession of Katanga at an end, and said he had acted under
Paragraph A.1 of the Security Council Resolution of the twenty-
first of February which authorized "the use of force if necessary
in the last resort" for the prevention of civil war. The representative claimed that the actions of Mr. Moïse Tshombe's
Government, including the use of foreign mercenaries and its
mass persecution of Katangese loyal to the Central Government
created a situation justifying action under Paragraph A.1.
Fighting continues in Elisabethville and European residents
report attacks by U.N. forces on hospitals and ambulances,
brutalities against missionaries, rapes of nuns, and other atroci-
ties by Gurkha troops. The present whereabouts of Mr. Moïse
Tshombe are not known.

(*Spotlight on* TSHOMBE *and* BRITISH CONSUL)

TSHOMBE

(*Agitated*)

Mr. Consul. I am a man of peace, not a man of war. The
other day, when the United Nations arrested the Belgian officers, what did I say? I said, "I bow to the United Nations,"
and so I did. I bowed. Everything was very nice. And then
what did you say? You said, "Moïse! Don't bow!" You said,
"Moïse, if you leave, my friends will lose all their copper, here
and in Rhodesia." You said, "Moïse, stand up to the United
Nations!" You said, "We will make it worth your while." You
said, "You will see, it will be safe — Great Britain, big important power, United Nations silly business." So I said, "O.K.
Let us defy United Nations." So what happens? Look at it, Mr.
Consul! I tell you this: I have had enough. United Nations
promise me personal safety just now. I have just to give up
secession. You ask me which means most to me, personal safety

or secession? Listen, Mr. Consul, I am not like all these crazy people mixed up in this business. I am sane. So I say personal safety. I make deal with U.N. But I want you to be there in case the Indians try to shoot me.

CONSUL

(*Somewhat inarticulately*)

Mr. President . . . Quite frankly . . . as far as your personal safety is concerned . . . Rhodesia is the best place for you . . . we can guarantee you will be safe . . . and comfortable . . . and you don't have to give up anything . . . just until this thing blows over. You risk nothing. If things go badly, you are safe . . . and you have . . . your investments. If things go well, you return to Elisabethville as a hero. What can you lose?

TSHOMBE

(*Suspiciously*)

What would I have to do?

CONSUL

Nothing much . . . one little talk on the radio . . . after that you can take it easy. Have a chat with Welensky. He gets on well with . . . Well, guest of H.M.G., of course. All that sort of thing.

TSHOMBE

All very well, but how do I get there? It's thirty miles to the border. The road is full of Indians, Irish, Baluba . . . I might get killed . . .

CONSUL

Mr. President, guarantee safety . . . Personally accompany

[176]

. . . Own car . . . Diplomatic immunity . . . Person of an
Envoy Sacred. United Nations obliged respect British flag . . .
All right, Mr. Tshombe?

TSHOMBE
(*Smiles*)

All right, Mr. Consul.

(*They rise. The* CONSUL *picks up a large Union Jack and
drapes it over* TSHOMBE. *He then leads* TSHOMBE *by the
hand towards the armchair near the placard "Ndola" at the
white line. The U.N. soldier salutes the flag. The* CONSUL
seats TSHOMBE *in the chair. Then he removes flag from*
TSHOMBE *and drapes it over back of chair. He hands*
TSHOMBE *a cigar which* TSHOMBE *lights, smiling. They
shake hands. Exit* CONSUL)

RADIO

Breaking his security silence, Mr. Moïse Tshombe from his
headquarters "somewhere in Katanga" today declared war on
the United Nations. We are determined, he said, to die to the
last man, rather than yield to the criminal aggression of the
world organization. The battle for Elisabethville continues.

(COLONEL ZBYRE *fires three shots in the air.* TSHOMBE
shakes the ash from his cigar and appears to doze)
(*Spotlight on* HAMMARSKJÖLD *and* REPORTER)

REPORTER

Secretary-General, your representative in Elisabethville is
quoted as having declared the secession of Katanga at an end.
How do you reconcile this with your own repeated statements
that the United Nations does not intervene in the internal affairs of the Congo?

[177]

HAMMARSKJÖLD

My representative must have been misquoted. The United Nations does not intervene in the internal affairs of the Congo. The United Nations action, which is essentially defensive, is not directed against Mr. Tshombe's Government. We are anxious to regain contact with Mr. Tshombe . . .

RADIO

(Repeats)

. . . United Nations action which is essentially defensive is not directed against Mr. Tshombe's Government. We are anxious to regain contact with Mr. Tshombe . . .

(Spotlight on AUGE *and* TAMWORTH*)*

TAMWORTH

Essentially defensive . . . indeed! What do you make of that, Agénor?

AUGE

What else can they say? Their little coup would have been very nice if they could have caught Moïse. But thanks to the spirited action of the worthy representative of Great Britain, they didn't catch Moïse. Moïse has been spared to lead on his white horse the crusade of his ancient nation against Communism, and so on . . . Causing cold feet in Washington. And when Washington gets cold feet, the United Nations loses a few toes. I think Hammarskjöld must be very nearly at the point where he will see that the service of his great ideal requires, once more, the dumping of some of his pals. Just one more turn of the screw, and I think we'll see Moïse restored to the throne of his ancestors, like Louis XVIII. Fragile things, restorations, of course, but they serve their turn. If Hammar-

skjöld really wants to make contact with Tshombe, why don't
we help him? Beowulf, I think in the interest of peace you
ought to go to Leopoldville . . .

(*As* TAMWORTH *starts to move toward Leopoldville, the
spotlight turns on* MUNONGO *and* ZBYRE. ZBYRE *is cleaning a
revolver,* MUNONGO *playing with a bayonet*)

MUNONGO

Alcibiade!

ZBYRE

Godefroid?

MUNONGO

I smell traitors.

ZBYRE
(*Looks around*)

Where?

MUNONGO

Tshombe. The Belgians. The English. They want to do a
deal with the U.N.

ZBYRE

The U.N.? Twenty kilos of plastique. Poff! (*He throws up
his arms*)

MUNONGO

We need a victim. *Oui, il me faut une victime* . . . Since
Lumumba — it is too long a time without blood . . . Alcibiade! Do you really hate the Swede?

ZBYRE

All French patriots hate him. All but Communists, like de
Gaulle. Hammarskjöld betrayed our Indochina. He betrayed
our Algeria. Betrayed at Suez, betrayed at Bizerta. We have
an account to regulate. So certainly. We kidnip. We kill. But is
this the time? They say he want make peace. So let him make
peace. We kill him after. What difference?

MUNONGO

If they make peace we shall have to make you leave. Peace
means doing what the Americans want. Americans don't want
you. You are too noisy, too bloody, too wicked. They want little
grocers like Moïse, and any killing to be done very quiet. So
peace means you are thrown out . . . So if you want Hammarskjöld, now is your best chance . . .

ZBYRE

Are you sure we must go if peace . . .

MUNONGO

Of course. Peace is American.

ZBYRE

Very good . . . The best is kidnipping. The kidnipping in
the air, like Ben Bella. For this we have specialists. About
kidnipping, the strong thing is that *after* you can decide. With
essessination is no after. But with kidnipping you can have
essessination after. Or other things as you wish. Without a
doubt is the kidnipping.

(*Spotlight on* TAMWORTH *and* HAMMARSKJÖLD)

TAMWORTH

Mr. Secretary-General, I hope you will believe me when I say

[180]

I have long admired your work for peace. I am, indeed, if I may say so, among those who regard you as an example for our time. You will understand therefore that if I have come here at this moment it is not at all in a hostile or even critical spirit, nor is it simply in the course of my duties as a public man. I come as one who understands and supports your great work for peace, to warn you that that work is now in the greatest jeopardy.

HAMMARSKJÖLD

My dear Tamworth, your motives are above question. For the rest, my office obliges me to be attentive at all times, where the peace is in question.

TAMWORTH

Thank you, Mr. Secretary-General. Yours is a lonely path and one on which only urgent necessity could bring me to intrude . . . I have not come to talk to you about the Congo.

HAMMARSKJÖLD

No?

TAMWORTH

Or only about the Congo as a symptom. What a symptom it is! But still only a symptom of a much more grave malaise. I fear, Mr. Hammarskjöld, that there is something in man's nature that rejects peace, something that instinctively inclines towards self-destruction. In better times how I should have welcomed a chance to talk to you about that — about the ideas of Freud and Einstein on peace . . . There is no need for surprise, Mr. Hammarskjöld, we modern dukes are often quite cultivated people. But time presses; in practical terms the point

is that the forces which are now coming into action against the
United Nations are so formidable that they are capable of destroying the organization. You have already against you the
Soviet Union, whose hostility is implacable. You have also
aroused, shall I say, the alarm of large financial interests — with
which indeed I happen to be connected — and although both
the political concerns and the influence of such corporations are
grossly exaggerated, it remains none the less a fact of life that
their alarm is apt to be contagious . . . The United Nations,
as you know, is getting a very bad press throughout both the
Western and the Communist worlds — a most unfortunate
coincidence . . . In Washington influential congressmen of
both parties have given vent to their indignation, in somewhat
turgid terms. The governments of Western Europe have already clearly marked their disapproval. The Government of
Great Britain has just exhibited some preliminary signs of disquiet.

HAMMARSKJÖLD

Preliminary?

LANDRACE

Yes, unless the Katanga enterprise of your subordinates can
be speedily and peacefully liquidated, I have good reason to
believe that Her Majesty's Government will make plain its lack
of confidence in your interpretation of the Security Council
resolutions. You will then be faced with the open opposition of
three out of the four active permanent members of the Security
Council. It is true that the fourth is the most powerful: the
United States. But I know you do not delude yourself about
that; you know that the Western alliance is regarded there as
more important than Katanga, the Congo, or even the United

Nations. If necessary, they too would sacrifice you. To be blunt, Mr. Hammarskjöld, if events continue of their present course, your resignation will be required of you.

HAMMARSKJÖLD

I am prepared to resign whenever my tenure ceases to be of service.

TAMWORTH

And have you considered what effect your resignation, extracted in such circumstances, would have on the *office* of the Secretary-General, and on the future of the United Nations?

(*A pause*)

I see you have. Mr. Hammarskjöld, the present course — about which in itself I have no comment — leads to the crippling of the office of Secretary-General. If the Secretary-General — the world's mediator — is made negligible, one of the great safeguards is destroyed; the defenses of peace are weakened, the chances of thermonuclear war are significantly increased.

HAMMARSKJÖLD

(*Slowly*)

I had given thought to that . . . What surprises me is that you should have done so.

TAMWORTH

Mr. Hammarskjöld, if there is general war, a duke burns as well as anyone else. I am therefore, in my own way, a supporter of the United Nations. I am not impressed when my colleagues tell me that the United Nations is nonsense. After all, since it is nonsense that gets men into war, why should not nonsense keep them out of it?

HAMMARSKJÖLD

My dear Tamworth, I am afraid I am not a humorous man. Not ever, and especially not now. One of my enemies said of me in Sweden that I had a humorless twinkle in my eye. It is there now. I know what you represent and I know its force. I know the mechanisms of international politics, and I know that the force which you represent has now become adequate to check my forward movement; that here the pendulum begins to swing back. You are a humorous man and insulated against horror by your sense of the ridiculous, which is a sort of talisman, I suppose. You cannot imagine, then, the horror of being strapped to an international pendulum, at the moment when one knows that the backward swing has begun. When one hears the preliminary whirring for the next set of mechanical noises required by the new direction, which was also the last but one, and which must produce the same creaks, the same echoes, the same murmurs as did the last but one. And provoke the same ghost. To be a person that wants to die, but to live on for the sake of the office . . . like a sick fish keeping himself alive, for the sake of his shell, until his successor has attained the appropriate dimensions . . . Please tell me now, Tamworth, without either sympathy or philosophy, what has to be done?

TAMWORTH

You must see Mr. Tshombe. You must see him personally. And you must take the initiative in seeing him. And this must be known.

HAMMARSKJÖLD

Very well. I shall see him. But in the Congo — in Katanga if he wishes, at any rate in the Congo; not in the place where I think your friends are keeping him. I take it you can reach him?

TAMWORTH

Yes.
(Takes up the telephone)
(Spotlight on Tshombe, still in easy chair, reading illus-trated paper. The telephone beside him rings and he takes it up)

TAMWORTH

President Tshombe?

TSHOMBE

Yes. Who's this?

TAMWORTH

This is the Duke of Tamworth . . . A colleague of Baron d'Auge.

TSHOMBE

Of course. How is the Baron? What a charming man. And Madame la Baronne? Or was it?

TAMWORTH

Mr. Tshombe, Mr. Hammarskjöld wants to see you.

TSHOMBE
(Indifferently)

All right, any time.

TAMWORTH

He wants to see you in the Congo.

(*Tshombe laughs*)
The line is rather bad. What!

TSHOMBE

The Congo? With a war on? No bloody fear! I'm all right here.

TAMWORTH

Safe conduct could be arranged . . .

TSHOMBE

The last time I got a safe conduct, I spent three months in jug. *He* wants to see *me*, you say. I don't care whether I ever see him. He gives me a headache, anyway. So if he wants to see me he comes here. Or I tell you what. I'll meet him at Ndola. That's the nearest airport. Rhodesia side, of course.

TAMWORTH

Very well, President Tshombe. The Secretary-General will see you at Ndola on seventeenth September. To arrange the modalities for your peaceful return to your capital . . .
(*They replace telephones*)

HAMMARSKJÖLD

In Rhodesia?

TAMWORTH

He won't come here. And it is *you* who need to see him.

HAMMARSKJÖLD

So I see him in Rhodesia if I am to see him at all . . .
(*Spotlight on* TSHOMBE *and* MUNONGO *at their respective*

telephones. ZBYRE *is beside* MUNONGO, *who still holds his bayonet*)

TSHOMBE

Godefroid?

MUNONGO

Moïse!

TSHOMBE

Listen, Godefroid. That Swede. You know? He's coming to see me. He's throwing in the sponge! What do you think of that?

MUNONGO

Nothing. How is he traveling?

TSHOMBE

To Ndola airport. On the seventeenth. His own aircraft, I suppose — the DC–6.

MUNONGO

How many in the crew? How many passengers?

TSHOMBE

I don't know. What does it matter? The main thing is . . . (*He sits up suddenly. In a more urgent voice*) Godefroid! Godefroid! Are you there?

MUNONGO

Yes, Moïse; you sound excited. You should avoid excitement, you know.

[187]

TSHOMBE

Godefroid, for God's sake, no tricks! Godefroid! Godefroid! Please!

MUNONGO

(*Chuckles*)

Take it easy, Moïse — calm yourself. After all, *you* won't be on the plane.

(*Replaces telephone and embraces* COLONEL ZBYRE, *with whom he does a sort of war dance, then squats and drives his bayonet into the ground*)

Can you be sure of getting him alive?

ZBYRE

He presents himself favorable . . . Of course, you can never be sure. We got Ben Bella. We missed Salan. We got Moumié. We missed de Gaulle. We got Mattei. Yes, we missed de Gaulle . . . But here the terrain is, as you say, conducive . . . Congo is provincial and also unappetizing. But is first-rate terrain for essessination and also kidnipping.

MUNONGO

How, this time?

ZBYRE

Our boys in Leo know what they have to do, once they get the signal. If they can, they put specialist on board plane.

MUNONGO

Specialist in what?

ZBYRE

Kidnipping. The hijack. We have good man there — Roger

Gheyssels. It is a Fleming, of course. But is trained — knows job. We get him on plane. Hammarskjöld gets in. Flight toward Ndola. Very nice, very tranquil. Then, just preparing to land, Monsieur Gheyssels puts pistol on back of pilot's neck and he say very politely: "I am sorry, sir, there is a little changement in flight plan. It is not Ndola any more. It is Kolwezi — K-O-L-W-E-Z-I — Kolwezi." And pilot, he say: "But Kolwezi is in the hands of Tshombe mercenaries!" And maybe Gheyssels, if he has time he says: (*Strikes attitude*) "Those you call mercenaries, sir, are the last idealists, the last *chevalerie* of the age!" Or maybe he just push pistol harder in pilot's neck. So they do not land at Ndola. They do not meet all these nice bourgeois and English milords. They do not make nice deal. They land at Kolwezi and meet some very nasty pipple. You for example. Me for example . . .

(*They laugh*)

Of course, it may not work like that. Maybe someone just hits Gheyssels on the head and shoves him in the compartment with the valises. Or maybe Gheyssels must shoot pilot. Or maybe there is a big *bagarre* and they all crash. But are many chances for something interesting to happen.

MUNONGO

How can you be sure of getting him on board?

ZBYRE

(*Shakes head*)

Never sure, Godefroid, never sure. You want to be sure — then do not embark on kidnipping and essessination . . . But are good chances. Always remember, Godefroid, United Nations are all Kents!

[189]

MUNONGO

Tous des cons!

ZBYRE

C'est ça, Godefroid — *tous des cons!* Gheyssels he comes
with the blue hat and the blue armband. No one recognize him.
Hammarskjöld and his friends they think — an official from
Leopoldville. Officials from Leopoldville — they think he's
one of Hammarskjöld's men from New York. He will carry two
sets of papers accordingly . . . You may say it is not possible!
Great world organization does not make such mistakes! But it
does, Godefroid, it does . . . And if Gheyssels is caught, our
boys will try other ways. Some of the packages the plane carries may turn into not quite the packages they expect. And if
that fails there is always our little warplane, the Fouga
Magister. One way or other, Godefroid my friend, I would say
the chances *against* Mr. Hammarskjöld arriving at Ndola are
about three to one . . .

(*Spotlight on* HAMMARSKJÖLD *and* BONHAM)

BONHAM

The delay, sir, is on a security clearance. The guards have
picked up a member of the party who claims to be with you.
His papers seem to be in order, but I didn't know him.

HAMMARSKJÖLD

Let's have a look at him.

(BONHAM *signals and* GHEYSSELS *is brought in by two
U.N. guards. He is a powerfully built fair-haired young
man*)
Well?

CHEYSSELS

Sievers, sir . . . Dutch national . . . attached to ECOSOC
. . . Specialist in mining law . . . Dr. Bunche thought it might
be useful for you to have me when you meet Tshombe, as he'll
have mining people. Sent me on ahead and told me to join you
here.

BONHAM

It'll take a little while to check his story, sir. . .

HAMMARSKJÖLD
(*Slowly*)

We don't have the time, Bonham . . . there are some things
we must take on trust. And I think . . . someone did say something to me about something like this. It seems to me that I
have been half expecting this man since I came . . . (*To*
CHEYSSELS) Very well. It all seems to be in order . . . (*To
guards*) This man is here as the result of a decision on the
highest level . . . he is to proceed.
(*Guards release* CHEYSSELS)

CHEYSSELS

Thank you, sir. (*To guards*) My briefcase, please.

GUARD

Just a moment, sir, for routine inspection. It's locked. Have
you the key?

HAMMARSKJÖLD

Let him be, Guard. I have told you he is already cleared by
the highest authorities.

[191]

(GUARD *steps back.* GHEYSSELS *picks up his briefcase and walks up the ladder*)

(*To* BONHAM) Well, Bonham, hadn't we better go aboard ourselves?

BONHAM
(*Hesitantly*)

I've been thinking, sir, that perhaps I might be of more use in Leo . . . to assure liaison.

HAMMARSKJÖLD
(*Smiles*)

Liaison is already assured, Bonham. On the highest level, as I said. You and I are both part of a pattern of which this journey . . . draws the threads together. You know the French saying "Who says 'A' says 'B.'" We both said A, in our quite different accents, and now here is B. Which we have to say also. Leaving C to be said by someone else . . . So go aboard, Bonham. I'll follow you.

(BONHAM *mounts the ladder rather shakily. When he has disappeared,* HAMMARSKJÖLD *follows, with an assured step, his head held high*)

(AUGE, TAMWORTH *and* TSHOMBE *assemble at* "Ndola")

AUGE
Well, Mr. President, this is your apotheosis, is it not?

TSHOMBE
I don't know whether it's that, Baron. I thought it was my liver. My stomach has been upset ever since I talked to Munongo the other day.

AUGE

I failed to make myself clear, Mr. President. What I meant was: this is your finest hour . . .

TAMWORTH

I should say so. The Secretary-General of the world organization, the modern Holy Roman Emperor, traveling through the heart of Africa at the bidding of a . . . of an African statesman whose merits the world has too long sought to ignore.

AUGE

It is certainly a remarkable turn of events.
    (*The noise of an aircraft engine begins to be heard*)
Here he is. Just on time. Very proper. One doesn't keep a head of state waiting . . .
            (AUGE *and* TAMWORTH *laugh*)
There's the landing signal . . . I suppose we should go on to the tarmac . . . Or would it be better to wait here on the terrace and let him walk up to us here . . . Better do the magnanimous thing, I suppose . . . Good Lord . . . What do you make of that, Beowulf?

TAMWORTH

Something wrong with the approach, perhaps . . . He's going to try again . . . No . . . He seems to be just circling . . . What the hell?

TSHOMBE

Oh God, it must be the Fouga! I feel simply rotten. My head hurts. I would like to go back to the hotel.

TAMWORTH

Steady, Mr. President. This is probably the most important moment in your life. What happens now . . .

(*A brilliant flash, followed by an orange glow in the distance, which continues to be visible until the end of the act. A silence. Then a dull boom*)

TSHOMBE

Oh my God, they've done it! Oh Jesus, let's go quickly.

AUGE

(*Takes him by the elbow*)

Mr. President, this is quite understandable; your nerves are under considerable strain.

TSHOMBE

The crash! The crash! What are we going to say?

TAMWORTH

(*Slowly*)

It's not at all certain that there has been a crash. Tropical lightning . . . thunder . . .

AUGE

One sees bush fires like that almost every night during this season . . .

TAMWORTH

I think it's clear enough that the man has simply turned back. The left-wingers with him have been doing their best to get him to do just that.

TSHOMBE

It's all very well, but it's bound to come out.

AUGE

You are a little overwrought, Mr. President. I suggest you say nothing to the press.

TAMWORTH

I'll talk to the airport people and tell them to close down. It's quite clear the man's not coming. There's no point in specu- lating about the reasons . . . A man like that . . . Then let's all get some sleep.

(TSHOMBE *buries his face in his hands.* TAMWORTH *takes* AUGE *aside*)

TAMWORTH

What do you make of it?

AUGE

Crash obviously. Sabotage probably. A disaster certainly.

TAMWORTH

Disaster?

AUGE

For us, I mean. Same mechanism as Lumumba's death. More trouble with those damned ghosts, looking for revenge.

TAMWORTH

So what do you advise?

AUGE

Blandness, Beowulf. Agnosticism. Myopia. We didn't see the crash, so how can we see the ghosts? And, of course, we never at any time heard the name of Colonel Alcibiade Zbyre. The trouble with these hired murderers is that they never know when to stop.

TSHOMBE

(*Raises his head*)

What can I say? What am I to say? That I am deeply shocked?

AUGE

No, Mr. President, not now. You say nothing for the present. In the morning, when you hear the news for the first time, you will be deeply shocked. So shall we all.

(*They help* TSHOMBE *to his feet*)

CURTAIN

Appendix

Hammarskjöld's Role in Relation to
the Downfall and Death of Lumumba

It is not contested that Hammarskjöld's policy towards Katanga, culminating in his decision to bypass the Prime Minister of the Congo in order to negotiate direct on 12 August 1960 with the President of a seceding province of that country, and the use made of this in secessionist propaganda, were the factors that provoked Lumumba into his fatal step of calling for Russian aid, in order to transport his troops to Katanga; see Hoskyns, *The Congo Since Independence,* pp. 174–175 and 189–190; also Pierre Davister, *Katanga: Enjeu du Monde* (Brussels, 1960).* This interaction is dramatically interpreted in Acts I and II. Once Lumumba had called for Russian aid, and thereby alarmed the Americans, it is also not contested that all Western diplomats and key U.N. officials at least approved of Kasavubu's attempted coup, and of Mobutu's successful coup, against Lumumba. Andrew Tully, in *C.I.A.: the Inside Story* (New York, 1962), claimed that the Central Intelligence Agency "masterminded" these operations. This claim

---

* The Correspondence between Lumumba and Hammarskjöld after the latter's return from Elisabethville is in the Addenda to Security Council document S/4417.

— it is in Tully's book a claim, or boast, and not an accusation
— may perhaps be exaggerated, as Miss Hoskyns seems to
think; given the political conjuncture in the Congo at the time,
the inflammation of American opinion against Lumumba, and
the known functions of the C.I.A., there is nothing inherently
improbable in what Tully says. Miss Hoskyns adds (p. 201):

"But there is no doubt at all that senior ONUC [U.N. Operation in the Congo; French order of initials] officials knew several days beforehand what Kasavubu intended and that most
of them hoped fervently that he would succeed. Whether they
passed this information on to Hammarskjöld in New York is not
clear but it seems likely that they did!" *

Whether or not U.N. officials played a part in the shaping of
Kasavubu's coup, there is no doubt that they did what they
could to make the coup a success. The dramatized account of
their actions in Act III is closely related to Miss Hoskyns's
narrative. One of them stated that his action in closing the
airfields was taken not at Kasavubu's request, but in the interests of law and order. "Whatever the justification," Miss
Hoskyns drily comments, "his actions both then and on the following days [6 and 7 September] did in fact correspond exactly
with Kasavubu's requests, and it is hard to believe that this was
totally coincidental" (p. 202 n.8). That the closure of the airfields was selective, in an anti-Lumumba sense, is apparent
from the fact that Joseph Iléo, Kasavubu's Prime-Minister-
Designate in replacement of Lumumba, was able to take off
from Leopoldville to seek support in the provinces while

---

* In a footnote to this Miss Hoskyns quotes one "highly placed U.N.
official" as commenting afterwards: "We all knew beforehand and were
delighted." In another footnote she mentions as "perhaps significant" the
fact "that all U.N. personnel in Leopoldville were warned well before the
broadcast took place that for security reasons they should not go out that
evening."

Lundula and Kamitatu, two of Lumumba's key supporters were prevented from traveling by air from Stanleyville to Leopoldville (Hoskyns, p. 204). The U.N. closure of Leopoldville Radio and Kasavubu's use of Brazzaville Radio are matters of record. As regards the Mobutu coup — the decisive one — Miss Hoskyns notes that U.N. officials seem to have felt that Mobutu was "the kind of officer around whom the new army could be organized" (p. 213). She adds: "A large number of [Congolese soldiers] were at the beck and call of anyone who could give them money. To counter this [*sic*] Andrew Cordier, at the same time as he decided to close the radio and airports, agreed to make available a grant of money to pay the troops in Leopoldville. Pay parades at which the money was handed over took place on Saturday, 10 September. It was apparently agreed that Mobutu should be allowed to claim the credit for this payment, in the hope that it would help to build up his authority and increase the hold which he had on his men." *

Four days after this episode Mobutu carried out his coup, of which the significant features were the definitive ouster of Lumumba, the suppression of the Parliament — in which Lumumba still had a majority — and the expulsion of the Russian and Czech diplomatic missions.†

---

* "UN financial records show that 5 million Congolese francs were paid out by Kettani in September to soldiers in Leopoldville." General Kettani was Deputy Commander of the United Nations forces in the Congo at that time. (Hoskyns, p. 213 n.).

† Curiously, Lumumba had not merely foreseen the danger of a military coup, but had publicly named the exact figure required to produce such a coup. On 15 July 1960 — a little less than two months before Mobutu's coup — he warned the Chambre des Députés against confiding the portfolio of Defense to any single individual "who could be corrupted by 5,000,000 francs into instigating a military coup d'état." (Author's translation from French text — *La Pensée Politique de Patrice Lumumba*, ed. J. van Lierde, Paris 1963). In the event the portfolio of Defense turned out not to be indispensable.

Miss Hoskyns, with the caution proper to a historian, finds it "extremely difficult" . . . to reach any definite conclusion as to how far Mobutu had been "encouraged" by the Western powers or by the United Nations (p. 215). She does, however, go so far as to recognize "that, whatever the intention, the United Nations action in paying the Leopoldville troops on 10 September went a long way toward strengthening Mobutu's authority and making the coup possible* (p. 216).

While the historian must hesitate, lacking absolute proof, the dramatist may present the hypothesis which he finds most convincing. It requires no extravagant recourse to dramatic license to transform Miss Hoskyns's narrative, with some other elements, into Scene II, Act III of *Murderous Angels*.

Did Hammarskjöld, in New York, know what his representatives were doing in Leopoldville in his name? In private, Hammarskjöld conveyed the impression, to some of those who talked with him at this time, that he was shocked by the lengths to which his representatives had gone. But he never publicly disavowed them, and indeed he publicly accepted full responsibility for what his representatives had done, or rather for his own somewhat imprecise version of what they had done. He said he had not been consulted in advance about the U.N. decision to close the radio and the airport, but he took "full personal responsibility for what has been done on my behalf"; he was "convinced of the wisdom of [these] actions" and added that the role of the United Nations in the recent crisis had been one of "utter discretion and impartiality"; he said that the airports had been closed to all but United Nations op-

---

* The reader should note that Miss Hoskyns is not only a careful, and even cautious historian, but also a historian well disposed both to the U.N. and to ONUC.

erations.* He may not have known and certainly did not say, that these United Nations operations included the movements of Joseph Iléo, designated as Lumumba's successor (above). It was on the day on which the Security Council meeting addressed by Hammarskjöld closed that Joseph Mobutu paid to his troops the 5,000,000 francs of U.N. money which made possible his coup of four days later.

I find it hard to resist the conclusion that Hammarskjöld both understood and approved the general sense of his representatives' action even if he did not know — or perhaps wish to know — all the details. As the sense of their action was the political elimination of Patrice Lumumba, it is for this that Hammarskjöld, in substance though not in form, assumed "full personal responsibility."

What degree of responsibility did Hammarskjöld have for Lumumba's actual death? In the context of the Congo, it was clear that Lumumba was placed in physical jeopardy as a result of his political downfall; the forces he represented were such that his political enemies, in whose hands the United Nations had helped to place the power, could not afford to let him live; he was after all still regarded by thousands of Congolese, including the majority of members of Parliament, as the lawful Prime Minister. The United Nations protected him for a time, "at his residence" — i.e. as long as he kept out of politics. When he left his residence, and was apprehended by those who later handed him over to his murderers, the United Nations could have intervened to save him, but in fact washed its hands of him. "As Mr. Lumumba had left on his own responsibility, orders were served to U.N. troops to refrain from any interfer-

* Security Council Official Records: 896th meeting: 9–10 September 1960 (S/PV. 896).

ence in regard to Mr. Lumumba's movements or those of his official pursuers." * General Rikhye, senior U.N. military adviser, later informed the U.N. Committee of Enquiry into Lumumba's death that the instructions not to "provide intelligence to the pursuers or the pursued, had been rigidly obeyed." † In the light of these instructions — which were, if not drafted, at least known and approved by Hammarskjöld, and submitted by him to the Security Council and the General Assembly — the statement which Hammarskjöld later made to the Security Council, when he was accused of responsibility for Lumumba's death — makes strange reading:

"Mr. Lumumba escaped from his residence in a way unknown to the United Nations and travelled east, without any possibility for the United Nations to know where he was and thus without possibility for the Organization to give him protection. He was arrested out in the country without any possibility for the United Nations to intervene as it was not in control of the situation." ‡

He did not mention, at this stage, the fact that even if it had been possible for U.N. troops to give Lumumba protection they

---

* General Assembly document A/4614; Security Council document S/4571, Report dated 5 December 1960, from the Special Representative [Dayal] to the Secretary-General, submitted by the Secretary-General to the Assembly and Council. In Act III I represent Dayal as having wished to intervene, and Hammarskjöld as having overruled him. There is no specific documentary authority for this. It was well known however that Dayal had taken what was regarded as a "pro-Lumumba" position for which he was bitterly criticized in the Western press. It is also known that Hammarskjöld on occasion drafted, or redrafted, important "reports" released in the name of his subordinates. There are traces, in the Special Representative's report, of the Secretary-General's very distinctive style. Such reports can, of course, record compliance with instructions, which are not necessarily cited as such. In any case Hammarskjöld made it clear that these policies had his full approval.

† General Assembly document A/4964; Security Council document S/4976; 11 November, 1961.

‡ Security Council, 935th meeting, 15 February 1961; S/P.V. 935.

were under orders, which they "rigidly obeyed," to do nothing of the sort. And it seems, according to Miss Hoskyns, that U.N. troops *were* in a position to give such protection and were specifically ordered not to. Miss Hoskyns's account, which I have followed in the play (Act III) runs as follows:

"The United Nations troops on duty in this part of Kasai were Ghanaians. When the news came through of Lumumba's arrest their commanding officer requested permission to rescue him and place him under United Nations protection. Though according to most sources there was considerable debate as to whether anything could be done, his request was refused and the Ghanaians were given strict orders not to intervene." *

The Soviet Government, in a statement released on 14 February 1961 blamed Hammarskjöld, in violent language, for Lumumba's death:

"The murder of Patrice Lumumba and his companions in arms in the dungeons of Katanga is the culmination of Hammarskjöld's criminal activities. It's clear to every honest person throughout the world that the blood of Patrice Lumumba is on the hands of this henchman of the colonialists and cannot be removed." †

In reality, this was far from clear "to every honest person throughout the world." Not only Western opinion, but also at least official opinion in the poor countries,‡ rejected, with

---

* Hoskyns, *op. cit.*, p. 267. Miss Hoskyns acknowledges in her preface that "many of those who have assisted most with this book have done so with the proviso that they must remain anonymous." It may be assumed that her sources here are persons who served in the United Nations at the relevant time. She refrains from adverting to the fact that this account flatly contradicts the Secretary-General's statement of 15 February 1961 to the Security Council.

† Security Council document S/4704.

‡ Among African countries, Guinea alone followed the Soviet Union in condemning Hammarskjöld outright. Several other countries showed varying degrees of disquiet about his role.

[203]

varying emphasis, the Soviet condemnation of Hammarskjöld. In part, the very violence of the Soviet polemic, and the staleness of its rhetoric, defeated its purpose. Hammarskjöld had earned too much respect, had shown too clearly his high conception of his office and his mission, for anyone outside the Communist organizations to acquiesce easily in the Soviet Government's labeling of him as "a sorry lackey of the colonialists." * Yet it is clear from an examination of the records, and of the results of Miss Hoskyns's enquiries, that there was much more force in the Soviet contention about Hammarskjöld's role in relation to Lumumba, than appeared at the time. It is now clear that United Nations officials, covered by Hammarskjöld's authority, helped to secure Lumumba's political destruction, and deliberately refused to prevent the arrest which led to his physical destruction.

---

* *Ibid.* The indignation of black Americans, was, I believe, directed more against the policies of the U.S. Government than against Hammarskjöld. It was Stevenson, not Hammarskjöld, who was interrupted in the gallery demonstration of 15 February (S/PV 934).

Notes

ACT I. PROLOGUE

p. 8.   See Part II, Chapter XI, "La Journée du 30 Juin," of *Congo 1960*, Tome I, published by Les Dossiers du Centre de Recherche et d'Information Socio-Politiques (C.R.I.S.P.), Brussels. This gives (pp. 318–320) the full text of the King's speech; the version in the play consists of extracts from this text, literally translated; even the capitalization of *Our* and *Your* is the King's own.

p. 10.   Full text in C.R.I.S.P. *Congo 1960*, I, 323–324; the version in the play also consists of literally translated extracts from this text, which was based on a tape recording of Lumumba's spoken words.

p. 12.   The mutinies began on 4 and 5 July at Leopoldville and Thysville; *Congo 1960*, I, Part III, Chapter II; Catherine Hoskyns, *The Congo Since Independence* (Oxford, 1965), pp. 87 ff.

p. 12.   Belgian troops also intervened at Luluabourg and Matadi. The intervention at Elisabethville was the earliest: it took place at 6 A.M. on Sunday, 10 July. Tshombe proclaimed the independence of Katanga on the evening of Monday, 11 July (Hoskyns, *op. cit.*, pp. 96–99; see also Appendix.) The other interventions were to cover the evacuation of Europeans: that in Katanga aimed at a restoration of the situation (C.R.I.S.P., *Congo 1960*, II, 719).

p. 16.   The term "Mau Mau" was in use at this time among certain Western delegates at the U.N. General Assembly, in reference to the militant section of the African membership. "Less technically oriented": See Shirley Hazzard's entertaining and illuminating collection of United Nations stories, *People in Glass Houses: Portraits from Organization Life* (New York, 1967).

SCENE I

p. 24.   This scene is set at a time just before Hammarskjöld's visit to Elisabethville, which was announced on 10 August and took place on 12 August (Hoskyns, p. 171). The purpose of his visit was to negotiate the entry of United Nations troops to Katanga, so that the Belgian troops, still in occupation of the southern part of that province, might be withdrawn in accordance with a resolution adopted by the Security Council on 9 August (Hoskyns, pp. 169–170). Tshombe had set ten conditions — known to his admirers as *les dix commandements de Moïse* — on which he would admit U.N. troops; the most important of the conditions were noninterference in the internal affairs of Katanga; nonuse of "Communist" troops in Katanga; and refusal by the U.N. to supply means for entry of Central Government troops in Katanga (Hoskyns, *loc. cit.*; see also P. Davister, *Katanga Enjeu du Monde*, p. 146, and the present writer's *To Katanga and Back*, p. 90). For Hammarskjöld's attitude to the *dix commandements* see Note to p. 33, below. On his way to Elisabethville, Hammarskjöld stayed overnight in Leopoldville but "made no attempt to contact Lumumba" (Hoskyns, p. 171); see Appendix. The reason for this seems to have been that he knew Lumumba would insist on trying to accompany him to Elisabethville; Tshombe would not accept this, and Tshombe's position, with his Western backing, was still strong.

p. 25. The University of Elisabethville had been founded as a "free" or "lay" university; the Katanga authorities, however, regarded "socialists" and anticlericals as unreliable and preferred militant anti-Communist Catholics. This led to a sort of purge at the lay university — the deportation of the atheists of which Polycarpe speaks. See *To Katanga and Back*, p. 131.

p. 29. The verses are from Hammarskjöld's *Markings* (pp. 206–207). They are the last two quatrains of a poem in six quatrains beginning: "Roused from my idle dreams . . ." The poem is dated "July 7, 1960– Spring 1961," the period from the breakdown of order in the Congo to the Security Council meetings following the announcement of Lumumba's death.

p. 33. The Katanga Government agreed to allow U.N. forces into Katanga on certain conditions (see Note to p. 24, above). After Hammarskjöld's visit Katanga propaganda claimed he had accepted these conditions. Hammarskjöld denied he had accepted any conditions and gave his own interpretation (S/4417/Add 6) of the limitations implied by the relevant portion of the Security Council Resolution of 9 August (see Hoskyns, p. 171–176). The interpretation, and the immediate subsequent actions of the U.N., seem to have given both Tshombe and Lumumba the impression that most of the *dix commandements* were accepted. Miss Hoskyns says (p. 172) that "by the time Hammarskjöld left well-informed Belgians were saying that *tacitly* the Organization had accepted eight out of the ten commandments." The U.N. troops stationed in South Katanga were originally mainly white — Swedish and Irish — and Belgian troops were still in Katanga a year later. From Tshombe's point of view he had made the minimum concession necessary — agreement to entry of U.N. troops — but had safeguarded, as he thought, the essentials of Katanga's independence. This was a realistic assumption, until the murder of Lumumba and a change of government in the United States transformed the whole situation.

p. 34. "The indispensable Power": "The most important member behind the Congo operation was the United States without whose political, financial and logistical support the U.N. Force in the Congo would have collapsed" (Ernest W. Lefever, *Uncertain Mandate: Politics of the U.N. Congo Operation* [Baltimore, 1967], p. 30).

p. 35. "Deep African roots": For the European roots, see Davister; also *To Katanga and Back*, Chapter 4. "Moïse" Tshombe, b. 1917 near Kapanga, Katanga; son-in-law of the paramount chief of the Lunda, the Mwata Yamvo. President of the Conakat, the political movement approved by Belgian financial interests in Katanga; subsequently President of the Katanga Provincial Government; declared Katanga independent on 11 July 1960. "Godefroid" Munongo, grandson of the former paramount chief of Katanga, M'Siri; first President of Conakat; Minister of the Interior in the Katanga Government; see *To Katanga and Back, passim.* At the time of writing, Tshombe is a prisoner in Algeria and Munongo is reported to be a prisoner in Kinshasa (formerly Leopoldville).

SCENE II

p. 46. Davister (facing p. 80) has a photograph of Hammarskjöld flanked by Tshombe and Munongo "before the Katangese flag": in the background a white man in a white cassock holds a microphone.
p. 46. The Commentator's text is fictional, but reflects the reality of Katangese jubilation on this occasion (Davister, pp. 154–156). See also *To Katanga and Back,* pp. 91–92.

SCENE III

pp. 51, 53. For the view of the United Nations as a kind of institutionalized prayer, or "ritual and dramatic substitute for war," see the present writer's *The United Nations: Sacred Drama* (New York and London, 1968).
p. 54. Once the original apparent Great Power consensus began to break down the danger of a "Korea" or a "Spain" in the Congo began to emerge. "If the United Nations fails," U.S. Ambassador James Wadsworth warned the Security Council on 15 September, "there will be no alternatives to unilateral action by many parties with all the implications that this would have for Africa" (S/P.V. 902). Five months later Hammarskjöld, facing the Soviet onslaught after the announcement of Lumumba's death, specifically claimed that the U.N. in the Congo had averted an internationally backed civil war there: "I do not now hesitate to say that on more than one occasion the drift into a war with foreign-power intervention of the Korean or Spanish type was averted only thanks to the work done by the Organization basing itself on African solidarity" (15 February 1961; S/PV 935; para. 23).

ACT II

SCENE I

M. Pierre Duviver, Lumumba's *chef de cabinet,* tells us that "the Secretariat of the Prime Minister was far from being a model of organization" (C.R.I.S.P., *Congo 1960,* I, 330). M. Serge Michel, who worked with Lumumba at a later stage, gives the same impression in *Uhuru Lumumba* (Paris, 1962). See also Hoskyns, p. 188.
p. 65. On 15 August, after Hammarskjöld's return to Leopoldville from Elisabethville, Hammarskjöld and Lumumba did not meet but exchanged five letters: ". . . Lumumba's allegations became increasingly wild . . . Hammarskjöld's replies were brief and cold" (Hoskyns, p. 174). This correspondence is in Security Council document S/4417/Add 7.

p. 66. There is no evidence that Hammarskjöld sought to warn Lumumba. Miss Hoskyns (*loc. cit.*) says that he was "furiously angry" and "personally insulted" by the tone of Lumumba's letters. Hammarskjöld's biographer, Joseph Lash, states that at this moment Hammarskjöld became convinced that Lumumba was "an incipient dictator who in his drive for power was prepared to wreck the Congo and the United Nations" (*Dag Hammarskjöld* [London, 1962], p. 239). There is a certain irony in this as the real "incipient dictator" who dissolved the parliament which supported Lumumba, was Joseph Mobutu, whom the United Nations helped to power (see notes to pp. 92 and 100, below).

pp. 70–74. After the break with Hammarskjöld on 15 August, Lumumba decided that the Congo would have to be reunified by the Congolese Army, and sought and obtained Soviet aid to transport his troops to Katanga. The Soviet Union supplied a number of trucks — originally intended for ONUC — and seventeen Ilyushin transport planes. The planes began ferrying troops from Leopoldville to Luluabourg about 25 August (Hoskyns, p. 190).

p. 75. Lumumba was aware that his move in obtaining Russian aid was dangerous; he was warned against it by the Ghanaians in Leopoldville (Hoskyns, *loc. cit.*).

SCENE II. See note to p. 34, above.

By the end of August the American press was reporting the State Department as foreseeing "Communist domination" of the Congo (Hoskyns, p. 195). See also Appendix.

pp. 84–85. "Eyes wide open": An ambassador would be unlikely to speak in this vein, and it is improbable that those who deposed Lumumba made themselves conscious of what had to happen to him then. The Ambassador here makes explicit — for dramatic purposes — what was foreseeable but may not have been distinctly foreseen at this stage. Later, there was at least one diplomat who did not hesitate, while Lumumba still lived, to express the view that the situation in the Congo required Lumumba's death: "Chaos has its own logic." See *To Katanga and Back*, p. 134.

SCENE III. See Appendix.

p. 88. Kasavubu's speech consists of translated extracts from his actual speech, delivered at 8:15 on the evening of 5 September on Radio Leopoldville; text in C.R.I.S.P., *Congo 1960*, II, 818–819. Kasavubu referred to Lumumba as "*le Premier Bourgmestro*."

p. 89. Lumumba's speech is based on the text in C.R.I.S.P., *Congo 1960*, II, 820–821, of his speech on Radio Leopoldville at 9:40 P.M. on 5 September, one hour and twenty-five minutes after Kasavubu's speech.

p. 91. "There then," wrote the correspondent of *The Times*, "the United Nations stands, ostensibly in the middle as always but leaning perceptibly in one direction" (7 September). The *Christian Science Monitor* on the same day noted that the United Nations was "helping to oust Patrice

Lumumba from the premiership of the Congo." Later the *Libre Belgique* observed that "without the U.N. Lumumba would in a few hours have gained control" (15 September; Hoskyns, p. 208).

p. 92.   The radio was closed by the U.N. on 6 September; Lumumba's attempt to force his way in took place on 11 September; on 12 September the radio was reopened but Lumumba was arrested by Congolese troops, held for some hours and then released; on 13 September the Congolese Parliament, amid some confusion and possibly without a quorum, voted full powers to Lumumba; on September 14 Mobutu carried out his coup d'état (Hoskyns, pp. 205–206; 214; See also Appendix). The reopening of the radio was due to Dayal's intervention. Dayal took over from Cordier as head of ONUC and Special Representative in Leopoldville on 8 September. Before this change, however, Cordier, at the time when he had closed the radio and airports, had agreed "to make available a grant of money to pay the troops in Leopoldville . . . It was apparently agreed that Mobutu should be allowed to claim the credit for this payment, in the hope that it would help to build up his authority" (Hoskyns, p. 213). The pay parades at which this money was handed over took place on 10 September; thus the policy laid down by or through Cordier continued, even after Dayal had taken over, long enough to seal Lumumba's political fate.

p. 98.   Lumumba was a strong feminist, and processions of women carrying green branches were a feature of his movement.

p. 100.   "We have just paid . . .": In fact the payment was arranged by Cordier before his supersession by Dayal. See note to p. 92, above. This is the gist of Mobutu's speech as recorded in C.R.I.S.P., *Congo 1960*, II, 869. "Il ne s'agit pas d'un coup d'état militaire," said the Colonel, "mais plûtot d'une simple révolution pacifique; aucun militaire ne prendra le pouvoir." Mobutu's troops turned out the Parliament on 16 September, and the Soviet and Czech Embassies on 17 September.

p. 101, 103.   From September on, until his escape on the night of 27 November, Lumumba lived in the Prime Minister's residence; from 11 October on — when Congolese forces had tried to arrest him — there had been a "ring of ANC troops guarding the outside and United Nations troops in the garden preventing his arrest" (Hoskyns, p. 255). "Mr. Hammarskjöld will defend us publicly . . .": See Appendix.

ACT III

SCENE I.   See Appendix. Lumumba's escape took place on the night of 27 November 1960.

p. 109.   Lumumba's infant daughter died on 18 November in Switzerland, where she had been under treatment. In a communiqué issued on the day of his escape he mentioned "le fait que depuis sa naissance, je n'ai pas eu et je n'aurai plus jamais la possibilité de voir ma fille." (C.R.I.S.P. *Congo 1960*, II, 1053). Dayal's report (S/4571; para. 4) on Lumumba's escape mentions his request for air transport to Stanleyville to attend the funeral.

p. 112.   Stanleyville, the capital of Orientale Province, was Lumumba's political fief, and remained at this time under the control of his supporters. See note to p. 101, above. There had been clashes between Congolese troops and the U.N. (Tunisian) troops protecting Lumumba.

p. 113.   See note to p. 34, above.

SCENE II

p. 118.   See Appendix and Hoskyns, p. 267. Miss Hoskyns does not specifically state that the U.N. forces were "in sufficient strength to free Lumumba"; I think, however, that this is a legitimate inference from the fact that their commanding officer sought permission to free him. For Dayal's position, see Appendix.

p. 120.   The description of Lumumba after his arrest is as given in Dayal's report (S/4571).

p. 122.   Lumumba was transferred to Elisabethville on 17 January 1961. The U.N. report of his arrival in Elisabethville is in S/4688, p. 120. Hammarskjöld addressed two "personal messages" to Kasavubu, on 3 and 12 December, asking for a fair trial for Lumumba. He later addressed letters of similar tenor to Kasavubu again (19 and 20 January) and to Tshombe (19 January) (A/4964). By this time Lumumba was probably already dead.

SCENE III

p. 128.   It is not known exactly when Lumumba and his companions Okito and Mpolo were killed. The United Nations Commission of Investigation accepted as "substantially true" evidence suggesting that they were killed on the evening of 17 January "in the presence of high officials of the government of Katanga Province, namely Mr. Tshombe, Mr. Munongo and Mr. Kibwe . . ." (A/4964).

p. 129.   See Joseph A. Moloney's *With Captain Stairs to Katanga* (London, 1893). The missionary who told me the story about Munongo's father — which I mentioned in *To Katanga and Back* — was later warned to leave Katanga, and did leave, because Munongo wished to see him about the story. The missionary has forgiven me, but has asked me not to mention his name in any future book.

p. 129.   The account here given is based on evidence before the Commission of Investigation (A/4964) and on the account attributed to Lucas Samalenghe (who died of gunshot wounds in November 1961) in Serge Michel's *Uhuru Lumumba.*

p. 130.   "Chaos": See note to pp. 84–85, above.

p. 131.   "To let it go unannounced . . .": It was announced, by Godefroid Munongo, on 13 February 1961. Munongo said Lumumba and his companions had escaped from Elisabethville and been massacred by the inhabitants of a village which Munongo refused to name. He ended by saying: "People will accuse us of assassination. To this I have only one response: 'Prove it!' " (Hoskyns, p. 316; A/4964, p. 48). A journalist present at Munongo's press conference told the U.N. Commission of

Investigation that Munongo produced Lumumba's death certificate, which read as follows: "*I the undersigned* Dr. Pieters *hereby state that* Mr. Patrice Lumumba *died* in the jungle in Katanga" (A/4964, p. 49). The words underlined were the printed wording of a form.

ACT IV

See Appendix. The play changes some of the order of proceedings of the Council.

p. 135. The Soviet statement, reproduced in S/4704, accusing Hammarskjöld of responsibility for Lumumba's death and calling for his dismissal, was issued on 14 February 1961.

p. 136. Hammarskjöld's words here are part of the text of his statement to the Security Council on 15 February 1961 (S/P.V. 935).

p. 136. "Official pursuers": See Appendix.

p. 137. "Telegrams": The most violent messages were from the Communist countries, and from Guinea, but many African countries expressed shock and dismay and varying degrees of loss of confidence in the United Nations. See telegrams from Upper Volta (S/4697), Morocco (S/4698), Mali, (S/4705), Sudan (S/4731), Ethiopia (S/4736), etc.

pp. 138, 140. Stevenson spoke on 15 February, but before Hammarskjöld, not after him. His remarks here are part of the text of his statement to the Security Council (S/P.V. 935) and were interrupted by the gallery demonstration at the point indicated.

p. 145. "This sorry drama": The words quoted in the play are from Sekou Touré's telegram of 14 February 1961 to the Secretary-General (S/4703).

p. 158. The United States Government also feared that if the secession of Katanga was not brought to an end, more African countries might, in their resentment over Lumumba's murder, recognize the Lumumbist-Gizenga Government in Stanleyville, as the United Arab Republic and Guinea did on 14 and 15 February (Hoskyns, p. 324). Paradoxically, U.S. fear of a "Central African Cuba" in Stanleyville helped to induce the U.S. to put pressure on "staunchly anti-Communist" Katanga, as part of the effort to retain "middle-of-the-road" Afro-Asian support. "Draft resolution": This became the Security Council Resolution of 21 February 1961, the turning point of the U.N. operation in the Congo, and the beginning of serious U.N. pressure on Katanga. See *To Katanga and Back.*

p. 161. "I've read a book of his": It was Professor Herbert Tingsten, former editor of the *Dagens Nyheter* and a severe critic of Hammarskjöld, who sent Hammarskjöld my book *Maria Cross.*

p. 162. See *To Katanga and Back, passim.*

ACT V

On 28 August 1961 Operation RUMPUNCH was carried out in Katanga, involving the mass arrest and expulsion by the United Nations of the Belgian and some other foreign officers of the Katanga gendarmerie. Some of the foreign officers, including a group of French rightist officers, escaped the dragnet. See *To Katanga and Back*, Chapter 13; Hoskyns, pp. 404–407.

SCENE II

p. 174.   The opening of Operation MORTHOR. See *To Katanga and Back*, Chapter 15; Hoskyns, pp. 410–435.

p. 176.   "Rhodesia is the best place for you": See *To Katanga and Back*, pp. 256–257; Hoskyns, p. 420.

p. 178.   "Essentially defensive": This is the thesis of Security Council document S/4940, a misleading document; see *To Katanga and Back*, Chapter 15. Miss Hoskyns (p. 422) says that Hammarskjöld decided "that a certain amount of covering up was necessary if the edifice which he had been building for so many years was not to crumble and the whole future of the Organization be put in jeopardy."

p. 179.   André Crémer, a Belgian gangster in Munongo's employment — later reported killed trying to escape from U.N. custody in Leopoldville — reported Munongo as having used to him, on an earlier occasion, the words *"il me faut une victime"*: there is independent confirmation of the assassination attempt organized by Crémer that followed this notification (*To Katanga and Back*, p. 234). The views here attributed to Zbyre were prevalent among the French warriors in Katanga at this time.

p. 184.   "Humorless twinkle": The phrase is Professor Herbert Tingsten's.

p. 186.   "In jug": Tshombe was arrested at Coquilhatville in April 1961; he was released in June. He was in the habit of referring with bitterness to the violation of his safe conduct at Coquilhatville.

p. 188.   The kidnapping plot in the play is based on the account in *Notre Guerre au Katanga* by Roger Trinquier, Jacques Duchemin and Bailly (Paris, 1963). Colonel Trinquier and M. Duchemin were advisers to Tshombe on military matters, at different times. The kidnapping story is Duchemin's. *Notre Guerre au Katanga* was published later than the Report of the U.N. Commission of Investigation into the circumstances of Hammarskjöld's death (A/5069, 24 April 1962). Stories had, however, already been in circulation, to the effect that an extra man had been aboard. The U.N. Report (para. 132) dismisses this rumor in the following words:

"As another possibility of internal interference the Commission notes the sensational story carried in several newspapers in some countries during January 1962 to the effect that a seventeenth man boarded the aircraft at Leopoldville for the purpose of hi-jacking it. The story speculated that the crash occurred when this man tried to take over the aircraft from the pilot. While this story falls clearly in the category of rumor, the Commission carefully investigated whether or not it was true. Dr. Linner and others who saw the plane take off from Leopoldville testified that they knew or were introduced to all persons who went aboard. Moreover, Dr. Ross considered the possibility of there having been a seventeenth body in the wreckage unlikely in the extreme, while the police, who did not know how many persons were aboard, examined the scene of the crash in order to discover if anyone had wandered into the bush, but found no trace of this."

The equally "sensational" story of the air kidnapping of Ben Bella some years before had been true, and curiously enough the man whom Hammarskjöld was flying to meet at Ndola was himself to be the victim of a sensational air kidnapping six years later. That security at Leopoldville airport was far from tight appears from another part of the Report (para. 81) which states:

"The Commission notes with regret and concern that in the afternoon of 17 September SE-BDY [the Secretary General's plane] remained for several hours unguarded and unattended on the tarmac of the airport. The evidence before the Commission shows that a person wishing to sabotage the aircraft might have gained access to it without being detected. The Commission considers that its terms of reference do not require it to pass judgment on individual responsibilties for the lack of special security measures with respect to the Secretary-General's plane at the Leopoldville airport, but it must be observed that necessary co-ordination appears to have been lacking. In this connection the evidence showed that while certain ONUC officials who should have been informed of the proposed flight were not so informed, other ONUC personnel not directly concerned had heard it discussed."

From this, it appears within the bounds of possibility that "the seventeenth man" could have been sitting inside the plane — in the lavatory for example — while Dr. Linner and his colleagues were being introduced, on the tarmac, to those of the sixteen whom they did not already know.

One might expect that the medical evidence would show definitely how many bodies there were but it does not quite do so; "unlikely in the extreme" is less than conclusive. The only on-the-spot medical investigation seems to have been that carried out on behalf of the Rhodesian Board of Investigation; the Dr. Ross named in the report was Forensic Pathologist to the then Federal Government of Rhodesia and Nyasaland;* the "Police" mentioned in the report were the Rhodesian police. The Rhodesian Government had an obvious and strong interest in a "pure accident" finding, and its terms of reference actually directed it to inquire into the causes of "the accident near Ndola." It is unfortunate that the original inquiry should have been solely in the hands of persons for whom the hypothesis that it might not have been an accident was excluded *a priori*.

The story of the kidnapping attempt no longer "falls clearly into the category of rumor," since it has been proclaimed as an exploit of Tshombe's forces by the person who was at the time Under Secretary for Defense in the Katanga Government, responsible for the forces in question — Jacques Duchemin. Duchemin names the person who, according to his story, was to carry out the exploit: Roger Gheyssels, a Belgian born in Katanga.

Unlike the Rhodesian Board of Investigation, whose "accident" finding

---

* A/5069/Add I, Annex VII. This Rhodesian report also affirms that "confident identification of all bodies was made" and concludes that "no medical cause for this accident has been found and there exists no evidence of sabotage."

was already inscribed in its terms of reference, the United Nations Commission of Investigation reached no conclusion; it found no evidence of foul play and no convincing cause for an accident; it therefore left the question open. As far as I am aware no attempt has been made to inquire into the question of whether any basis in fact exists for the assertions made by Duchemin in *Notre Guerre au Katanga,* in the year following the return by the United Nations Commission of an "open verdict."

p. 191.   The idea of Hammarskjöld's "acceptance" of Gheyssels's mission is based on the sacrificial element in *Markings,* combined with the political situation at the time of Hammarskjöld's embarkation.

p. 193.   "The Fouga": A small Belgian-piloted training plane, which was at this time the only fighting aircraft in the Congo. The United Nations had at this time no warplanes. When Hammarskjöld's plane crashed, most people in Elisabethville immediately thought of "the Fouga."